ADIRONDACK EATS
RESTAURANT GUIDE

Matthew DeLaMater and Molly Irvine

Matt DeLaMater   *Molly Irvine*

Cold River Press
An Adirondack & Literary Imprint
Long Lake, NY

www.adirondackrestaurantguide.com

Copyright © 2011 | P. Matthew DeLaMater and Molly Irvine

ISBN: 978-061550369-1

First Printing, 2011
Designed | Printed | Produced in the United States of America
Printed by: InnerWorkings Inc., Grand Rapids, MI
Design: InnerWorkings PreMedia Group
Cover: Arne Limner
Maps: Arne Limner

REGIONAL MAP

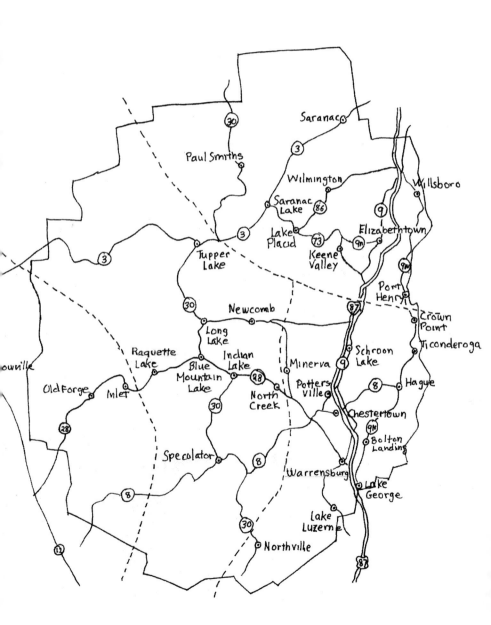

TABLE OF CONTENTS

INTRODUCTION

We love the Adirondacks; it is a magnificent and treasured region, full of natural beauty and abundant local character. To the thousands of people who come here to experience its splendor first-hand, we want to extend our welcome. At the simplest level, the goal of this guide is to match our readers—whether locals, seasonal residents, or occasional visitors—to a restaurant where they can have a successful dining experience. The good news, as we've found out during the long course of this first-time project, is that the Adirondacks—recently regarded as a culinary backwater—are rapidly improving in the variety and quality of food served. In the pages of this guide, we want to applaud the restaurants doing things well, and describe them so you can decide if they might be your kind of place too. We also want to help readers avoid the dining disasters that can spoil a hard-earned night out, an event that ultimately leaves a visitor's trip to our great park unnecessarily tarnished.

We began this project by polling both friends and strangers who are frequent Adirondack diners; it's a big place to cover, with over 9,000 square miles. We asked them where to go, what to get, and to rank their favorite places. From this local survey, we generated a list of about 70 restaurants that we would visit over the course of a year in order to select our Top 46 (one for each of the official High Peaks) featured reviews. Along the way, we know we missed a few gems, and, inevitably, some of the good ones that we did find will experience a decline before the next edition.

In evaluating a restaurant, we looked hard at both the quality of the food and the price. As fans of everything from a juicy hamburger to high-end foodie cuisine, we appreciate a quirky joint at least as much as a gourmet place, if not more. We hope our list reflects our diverse tastes, and offers some interesting choices. To enhance our range of response, we added a friend to our team who chose to remain anonymous, a person we refer to as Food Snob (for obvious reasons). Additionally, in the writing itself, we hoped to impart a feel for the restaurant's character and ambience, although atmosphere only went so far in making our list.

Most of the time, we were able to review in anonymity. In Long Lake, where we live, this was not possible, and we were probably known a couple of other times, but we did our best to be as fair as possible. It's obviously a subjective enterprise, but local consensus usually emerged rather clearly. While we hesitated before ranking our favorite Top 46 in order, ultimately, we did so hoping it would provoke some competition and discussion. We do not mean it to be a definitive evaluation.

Lastly, we hope our readers will take the time share their opinions. Let us know about your dining adventures, and please alert us when your experience is significantly different from ours. We look forward to hearing from you through our website at: www.adirondackrestaurantguide.com.

Matt DeLaMater

Molly Irvine

Food Snob

Special thanks to:

Karen and Bob Spicer, Carol and Jeb Irvine, Paul and Susan DeLaMater, Alex Roalsvig, Colleen Smith, Vickie Verner Sandiford, Lisa Ciniglia, Dustin Traynor, Antony and Andrea Dawson-Ellis, Scott Irvine, Victoria DeAngelis, Doug and Tricia DeLaMater, Todd Fisher, Jimmy Knowles, Kate Parent, Christine Campeau, Tommy Bissell, Casey Lemieux, Travis Collegian, John and Stephanie Lemieux, Elena Chechenkova, Jazen Reuss, Molly Stone, Rachel Pohl, Jan E. Belle, Sarah Gallagher, Kristi Lance, Jules Hosley, Katie Keller Slentz, Karrah Gereau, Natalie Nerney, Carrie Verner, Darren and Lola Linck, Dan and Kara Ott, Melanie Frost, Casey and Chris McDermott, Stephanie Howe Wells, Julie Anne Tellstone, Tammy Kitchen, Angie Donnelly Snye, Alex Harris, Marji Holton, Rachael Ball, Jason Folmsbee, Matt Newby, Katie Christianson, Melanie Marcone, John and Lori Hosley, Shari Keller, Joy Barcome, Becky Monty, Maureen Long, Ali Tribley, Carol Atkins, Suzanne Denney, Sarah Cardinali, Norm and Valerie Galvagni, Casey Beneduce, Bill and Phyllis Ryan, Brittany Obert, Tony Musso, Billay Sandiford, BJ Rehm, Amanda Helms, Cheyennea Huntley, Yod Roalsvig, Clay and Lauren Arsenault, Chris and Steph Hample, Tim and Erica Brzuszkiewicz, Kristin Zilliox, Colleen Coughlin, Hanna Bush, Ezra Crawford, Garland Walsh III, Hanna Bush, Bridgette Trudeau, Jaybay Hall, Andy Pauls, Brooke and Eric Hample, Joan Whittaker, Carol and Carmine Inserra, Lorisse and Jim Keating, Arne Rostad, Jane and Tom Bissell, Lauren Mosness, Justin Facto, Cassandra Mitchell, Chuck Frost, Bree Waite, Jade Stephenson, Julie Nealon, Kate and Marvin, and Patty Burgess.

Special thanks also to our Production Team at InnerWorkings: Mary Motta, Rinck Heule, Tiffany Sinkule, and Missy Goggins.

Adirondack Eats

CHALLENGES OF RUNNING AN ADIRONDACK RESTAURANT

In talking with many restaurant owners and chefs while researching this book, we thought we might share some insights into the challenges facing Adirondack restaurants. Emerson's famous quote about "a foolish consistency" being "the hobgoblin of little minds" clearly was not written about the dining industry; in that endeavor, consistency is everything. So those restaurants that succeed in being good and dependable all year round deserve particular commendation. Here's a brief outline of what they are up against, for your consideration as a customer.

1. Short Season

The Adirondacks are home to about 135,000 residents; 200,000 seasonal residents, and 7-10 million visitors each year. While Old Forge maybe the snowmobiling capital of the northeast, and Lake Placid and North Creek known as ski resorts, the rest of the Park relies on the summer vacation months.

Restaurants might go from serving 10-20 dinners on a Saturday in May to 100-200 on a July weekend night, a ten-fold ramp up, and a huge transition for the staff. Turning tables is a priority, things can get harried, and, yes, quality control can sometimes suffer. Owners and chefs often work seven days a week for two months straight. Meeting the demanding schedule with skill, grace and talent is no easy task.

2. Staffing

Since seasonal employees come and go, getting a new summer staff in place is an annual challenge. College students can readily find jobs in this area, but then head back to school early before the busy season is over. Many establishments have turned to hiring foreign help (Russians, Romanians, Poles, Serbs, etc); while generally very hard working, these students are shy about their language skills and unfamiliar with our service customs. They arrive days before the season starts, and are thrown in with little prep time.

3. Overworked Local Staff

Having survived yet another lean winter, many Adirondackers spend most of the summer working in the service industry. Most have multiple jobs, contractors by day, and bartenders by night, that sort of thing. While they are grateful for the influx of customers, they can get worn out or overwhelmed. Yet, don't underestimate their love of this region; that's why they stay. Many of these people are highly educated—more than one person has had the experience of finding their server from the night before giving a lecture at the museum the next day—so careful about being dismissive. Wait staff are often teachers, graduate students, and professionals trying to save money for the leaner months. At the same time, bad service and poor meals are inexcusable in a region that depends upon repeat tourism.

4. Suppliers

Needless to say, given the economy of scale, ordering deliveries of food in the off-season requires a crystal ball. Because demand is erratic, frozen food is often used to off-set wastage. Menus often change as a result, down-scaling occurs, and fresh daily specials simply aren't feasible. Good produce becomes scarce. While chefs would love to use local game and fish, New York health regulations make this practically impossible. The good news, on the other hand, is that more local suppliers and organic farms are emerging, a positive trend for those restaurants that experience a more steady fall and winter clientele. Many of the restaurants on our Top 46 List are taking advantage of these new sources of quality ingredients, and some are even growing their own herbs and vegetables.

5. Long Off-Season and Increasing Heat Bills

Most restaurants face yet another challenge when the high season ends. Knowing that for the remainder of the year they will be operating at a loss, owners must weigh shortening hours of operation, adding days off, cutting employees, and trying to keep the good ones that they have. Mother Nature is unpredictable yet yields a heavy influence—the right amount of snow (and ice on the lakes) makes or breaks the ski and snowmobile season. Naturally, a brutally cold winter and rising fuel costs in 2010 and 2011 really hit businesses hard. Since family operations are quite common, layoffs weigh heavily upon owners. Some owners borrow money to stay open rather than face giving the pink slip to friends and relatives. On top of that, the local customer base wants inexpensive food and large portions, requiring a shift in focus. Keeping chef's happy turning out burgers, pizza and chicken *parmigiana* isn't easy either. The restaurants that manage to happily accommodate visitors and residents year round deserve a lot of respect.

6. The Recession

Like everywhere in America, the recession has meant a decline in consumer spending. But here, the recession also represents an opportunity. As people continue to cut back on travel abroad, and with the dollar in a tailspin, Adirondackers are hoping to attract more tourists from throughout the northeast region. It may be a difficult place to run a business, but, for visitors, the Adirondacks represent an awful lot of bucolic beauty at a very affordable vacation price. Owners now face the task of bringing customers here, and making sure that they have a good experience.

Hopefully, this partial outline gives readers a glimpse into the other side of things.

USING THIS GUIDE

Featured Reviews

Each of the four regions—North, South/East, Central, and West—has its own chapter. We begin these chapters with our featured reviews, ranked in order of preference. Our number one favorite restaurant in the North region is Liquids and Solids; South/East is The Farmhouse on Top of the World, etc. The complete rankings of our Top 46, with all regions evaluated together, can be found after the Regional Chapters, on page 167.

Local Lowdown

Each region also includes a section called the Local Lowdown, which has brief reviews on dozens more restaurants, organized by town. We've included, whenever possible, addresses, phone numbers, and viable website listings. Review comments are drawn mostly from our surveys and others are from our visits.

The Final Top 46 Favorite List

Our overall Top 46 Favorite list is based almost entirely on our own experiences during review visits, but local surveys also have a part to play. It is tough to completely evaluate a restaurant based only on one or two experiences. It's also impossible to make a set of meaningful objective benchmarks. Thus, theses rankings are subjective.

Remember that once in awhile, everybody has an off night—or a particularly great night—which may skew reviews from a typical experience. Your opinion may vary from ours (please contact us about your experiences when you feel we've missed something; we're always looking for tips). And don't forget that creating a Top 46 listing that includes high-end restaurants, bars, as well as hamburger joints—well, it's not that easy.

NORTH REGION:

Lake Placid, Saranac Lake, and Keene Valley

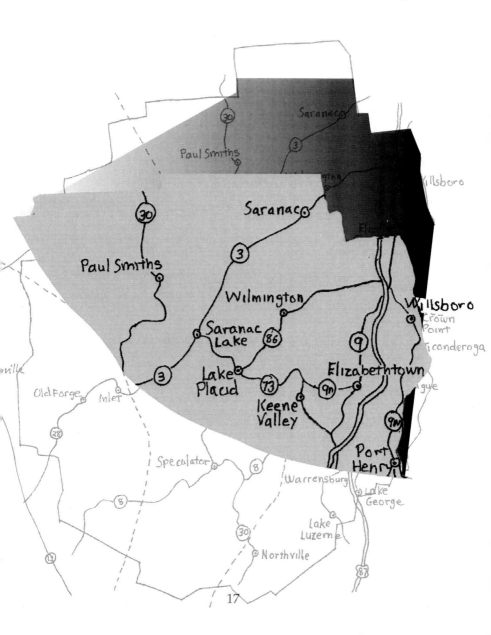

Featured Reviews:

1. Liquids and Solids (Lake Placid, April 2011)

Sure, some people are put off by the name. However, since June of 2010, Liquids and Solids has successfully brought the small plate/ big plate concept to Lake Placid. Located a bit off the beaten path in a former dive bar known as The Handlebar, it is deservedly gaining an enthusiastic following of locals and seasonal residents. It's a gastro-pub with a no frills atmosphere, informal and fun, with the menu printed out in single sheets and attached to a clipboard, while the wine and beer lists hang behind the bar written on remnants of recycled paper bags. Yet, don't be fooled, for the food and drinks here are complex and imaginative. Chef Tim Loomis a graduate of Paul Smith's in Saranac, has made a remarkable first year debut, with a constantly modified menu that inspires repeat visits. If you have any sort of adventure in your palate, you can expect an entertaining evening sampling a variety of unusual and intriguing combinations that highlight local and sustainable products.

The first time we went we ate right at the bar. For those who like an Olympian challenge, try to get co-owner Keegan to laugh while she intently pours cocktails; certainly her drinks are at least worthy of a gold or silver in the world of Adirondack mixology, and some regulars swear she's not a bartender but rather an alchemist. We liked the "Ward111"—and not just because it sounds like the name of a Chekov story—but rather for its balanced blend of scotch, vermouth, lemon, honey, and bitters, served foamy topped with egg whites, a nice old-school twist. The "Smoked Ale" is inventive and spicy, the "Lavundula" a great summer selection featuring raspberry puree and lavender syrup, and the Balsamic Fizz Vodka sounds strange but proved remarkably delicious. They've got a good selection of beers, and much to our delight, brought out a secret stash of SmuttyNose Old Dog Brown Ale, arguably the most perfect microbrew produced in this country. For us, the temptations of the cocktails and beers overshadowed the wine selections.

You might want to start with the beet and goat cheese salad, light, clean, delightful. The grilled calamari came out tender and flavorful, the risotto and beans, with chimichurri shrimp, also worked well. *Poutine*, a Quebecois specialty featuring French fries smothered in gravy, met with high marks from our own French-Canadian guest; the beef gravy and cheese curd tasted especially pleasing. Some of the regulars threatened to hold us hostage if we didn't try the L&S double burger (replete with its own secret sauce, and only seven bucks). Served on a focacia-like bun, the meat came out tender and juicy, and, again, the use of cheese curd in the sauce completed a remarkable ensemble. Yes, all agreed that this might be the best burger in the North Country. And yet, on our second visit, this time with a large party, the Tuna B.L.T., barely seared yellowfin tuna served on an English muffin—with bacon jam, tomato, aioli and capers—may have stolen the show. Food Snob enjoyed his rather non-traditional bouillabaisse, particularly the featured rock shrimp, all the while boring the far end of the table with comparisons of the fish stews served in various parts of France ("in Brittany the color is almost green, I suppose from the saffron, and comes with croutons and aioli...."). The French fries should not be overlooked, crisp, peppery, ask for the homemade ketchup to go with them. The desserts vary frequently, are generally excellent, the apple fritter is recommended, while the blackberry Napoleon with banana rosemary sauce proved memorable.

We don't always get to test a restaurant with a large party, and, in this case, the service proved excellent, the dishes and drinks kept coming at a good pace, and our server remained all smiles even when we sheepishly plunked down six different credit cards for our party of ten. Oh yeah, it's more than reasonably priced, and given the overall quality, represents a real value in a town known as the most pricey spot in the mountains.

2. Chair Six (Lake Placid, June 2011)

Talk to enough overworked chefs, and a common dream repeats itself. It's a vision of running the Great Good Small Restaurant, consisting of a handful of tables, a carefully selected menu, the time to lavish attention to the details of each dish, everything fresh, natural, often local—the perfect venue for a return to the passionate joy of cooking. Talk to enough foodies, and they're looking for exactly the same thing.

Yes, Chair Six is just the place for the marriage of such dreams. We'd driven past it more than once, barely noticing it, and without the sign, we assumed it was just another house in the neighborhood, or some kind of ski shop (in fact, the breakfasts are highly regarded in the skier community). Offering lunch and dinner as well to customers, we booked an evening table for the big show. With only six interior tables arranged in a tight cozy setting, reservations are a must.

We went on Wednesday night, where chef/owner Charlie Levitz features a 25 dollar three-course menu; each course offers one of four selections. We started with the Israeli couscous, with spring vegetables and warm artisan feta custard. The firm texture of the couscous, combined with the velvety tanginess of the mild feta, well, not only is this a must order dish, but arguably the best opener we'd had all tour. The classic beet salad with arugula and goat cheese—here we are going to nit-pick—was good, but could have used more *chèvre* and the produce was virtually uncut. It just didn't rank in the same league as the couscous.

Food Snob went with the fresh pasta dish, which featured a red pepper sauce, fiddlehead ferns, wild ramps, and oven-roasted tomatoes. Truly excellent, we asked for extra bread to sop up every bit of the sauce. The rest of us took the rare opportunity to get soft shell crab, dusted in cornmeal then fried, and served with a fresh roasted sweet corn salsa. The crab was sweet and

21

tender, and the accompanying corn, clearly just cut from the cob, represented a beautiful friendship.

For dessert, the perfectly fine *crème brulee* came with a glassy clear thick crust, a neat trick, while the strawberry-rhubarb "pot pie" had just the right balance of tartness and sweetness.

Now, clearly, Chair Six represents one of the top tier restaurants in the Adirondacks. However, inarguably, the Wednesday night special, given the price and quality, makes it our favorite restaurant in the Park on that particular evening.

3. Caffé Rustica (Lake Placid, September 2010)

Most of us, admittedly, tend to hesitate before being lured into restaurants that are located in a strip mall. Then we heard that the pizzas were thin crust and made in a wood-fire brick oven, and, well, it became a must stop.

First of all, the ambience of Caffé Rustica is unexpectedly warm and even, dare say, romantic; the interior decorator managed to create a space where you immediately forget that just across the parking lot sits the Price Chopper. Just outside the entrance, the crackling patio fireplace takes the chill off the Adirondack nights, and the smoky scent serves as a sort of transitory mood enhancer before you go inside. Prior to expansion a year ago, on crowded nights, we often enjoyed eating right at the bar, where you can peer into the semi-open kitchen and see wonderful things going on. The tables are cozy and intimate, the colors warm, the lighting subtle, and the service has generally been good to excellent, with the staff willing to explain the dishes, make suggestions, and help out with the wine pairings from a well-selected list.

Invariably, after having some crusty bread dipped in balsamic and olive oil, we start with the fried goat cheese appetizer and usually fight over it. Then we split one of the special salads available for that evening, which usually features fresh local ingredients and wonderful dressings. Chef Kevin Gregg, a graduate of the Culinary Institute of America, also brings some fine daily chalkboard entrees, the pan-seared sea bass being a recent memorable selection, and generally speaking, the seafood selections are almost always terrific, as is the risotto. Food Snob, who "prefers Northern Italian" is particularly partial to Rustica's tender rendition of Chicken Saltimbocca, a sautéed chicken dish with prosciutto, Parmesan, a little white wine sauce, all successfully seasoned with a bold amount of fresh sage. ("*Saltimbocca*" supposedly means "jump into your mouth" in Italian. Don't ask about *Puttanesca*.) For those looking for the best bargain on the menu, the pizzas make a fine choice, and are of the thin crust variety and feature quality ingredients, with no Jersey shore greasiness so often prevalent here in the mountains.

Overall, the portions are generous, in line with local expectations and appetites; modest eaters will either share or find themselves taking food home. For urbanites, the prices seem moderate given the quantity and the quality; locals consider it a splurge on the relative scale of things. After the meal, the espresso pairs wonderfully with the tiramisu; they also had a rare treat, Hungarian *Tokaj*, the favored dessert wine of the Tsars and a legendary aphrodisiac— its unique tartness is worth experiencing once in your life, and its high anti-oxidant content can't hurt either.

Café Rustica ranks as the top Italian restaurant in the Placid region, and with its recent expansion, has not yet shown any signs of slipping (while making it easier to bring the family in early hours, or get a table on busy nights). Open for lunch and dinner, they don't take reservations.

4. Caribbean Cowboy (Lake Placid, July 2010)

Hidden away on the approaches to downtown Lake Placid, the Caribbean Cowboy is easy to drive right past even when you kind of know where to look for it. Situated behind the Sourdough Bread Company, with no lighted sign, the place can appear closed. So you might drive by it a few times (it's near the McDonalds) before finding the driveway that puts you in a fairly tight parking lot behind the restaurant.

Often jammed (no reservations, so be prepared to wait in season), the Caribbean Cowboy maintains a happy vibe even while cranking out dish after dish, and to best soak it all up try to get a table on the kitchen side, where you can see the chefs and serving staff at work. Some people aren't thrilled with the reggae, or the Island kitsch décor and the sort of "shack" ambience. However, we've found the environment infectiously upbeat, couldn't care less that there are no tablecloths, and, judging by the dancing and banter that goes on in the kitchen, we find this to be a place where the staff gets hyped up on the buzz of what they are doing— no Gordon Ramsey-esque yelling and tantrums here, no huffy, breathless service, no passive-aggression between the front and back of the house. The service has been consistently friendly, and we always appreciate servers who don't hesitate to weigh in and guide your selections (after all, it is always reassuring to know that a server eats where they work and likes it).

Given all this, why not start with one of the featured cocktails? The "Pain killer" is popular, but those who want to indulge their feminine side might prefer the "Funky Monkey," a tasty frozen chocolate/banana drink that avoids excessive sweetness.

The cuisine is unquestioningly inventive and, here's an overused word, eclectic. The progressive dishes draw their inspiration and rely on Caribbean styles and ingredients, while others draw from some Thai and Japanese influences, and oh yeah there's hummus and Moroccan *tagine* and other Mediterranean stuff, and with the various nightly specials, well, it's just tough to pin this place down. Some dishes are a definite fusion, and two perfect examples are the spinach and shrimp Fritters, spring rolls Jerk chicken, both generous appetizers we can endorse. Other dishes are fairly straight-forward, like the regular Jamaican Jerk chicken, which managed to be different and, frankly, among the better we've had anywhere.

The steak dishes and burger are the reason the place is called the Caribbean Cowboy rather than something like the "Jamaican Ninja." The Cowboy has justly earned a reputation for doing beef up right, and the marinated flank steak was probably the best item of the night. Vegetarians will not be disappointed either—here these dishes are featured and not just a reluctant afterthought— even inveterate meat-eaters have been seen stealing a few bites from their moralizing veggie eating friends.

The key lime pie, made on the premises, is a good dessert choice, but, given that even the appetizer portions are large, saving room can be a challenge.

Admittedly, this place has long been a staff favorite, and over the course of the last five years, we've had a series of good to great dining experiences here. Whether its date night, or family night, this is a place that can bring it.

5. Lisa G's (Lake Placid, September 2010)

Outside the oft-crowded downtown of Lake Placid, Lisa G's occupies the building of a former Opera House, a place that is reputedly haunted, and past which, in full view of the restaurant's inviting wooden deck, a rather picturesque little waterfall and stream (Chubb river) run past. Inside, the restaurant is split almost evenly into a bar section and a dining room, and the warm red and yellow colors that are so in vogue lately yield a very pleasant, tastefully lit, and relaxing ambience. It's easy to feel comfortable here, and the crowd seems to be a mix of locals and seasonal types who naturally have found their way here over time. (Yet, thankfully, the bar seems to lack the kind of annoying regulars who can be found festooned to a stool and largely holding court day after day, tramping as it were, on the last nerves of even the most patient bartender; the relative charm of local characters being often heavily dependent on the limits of exposure).

The bar is ample and comfortable, and features a few good drafts and wines, not to mention some rather interesting experiments in mixology. The Bloody Mary would make Harry's Bar proud, just the right amount of kick. The drinks are pricey but generally large, and some could easily be considered enough for two to tackle. In general, the combinations avoid excessive sweetness, and focus on some interesting ingredients such as ginger or balsamic which, overall, imparts an interesting edge. Getting mildly sloshed on some of these beauties is not an entirely unpleasant way to begin an evening.

We found our way here on the basis of several strong recommendations from residents and Placid restaurant folks. Insiders told us that the chicken wings were excellent, but, after having eaten enough chicken wings in the course of this book to satisfy a reasonable lifetimes' quotient, needless to say, well, we almost skipped it. That would have been a big mistake. Lisa herself brought us a sampler plate of the wing styles currently available, and, suffice it to say, that if a soundtrack were included in this book, we would now have to play some angelic choral fanfare before pronouncing these wings as the best we had all summer. In particular, the Greek style wings, cooked with a bit of lemon and seasoning, fried perfectly, when coupled with the homemade feta sauce, achieved a near Platonic level of ideal wing perfection. Sure, it's not the traditional Buffalo style, it won't set your mouth a-burning, and thus perhaps purists will consider this a violation, but damn they were good. The teriyaki wings, normally a choice much dreaded by Food Snob, who reviles the sickly sweet packaged taste seemingly ubiquitous to all things "teriyaki," was a close second.

Having passed the chicken wing test with more than aplomb, Lisa's next request came from our barbecue specialist, who rather imperiously wanted a free sample of the pulled pork barbecue. With a graciousness that is her hallmark, and in a friendly tone that greatly mollified this difficult reviewer, Lisa soon produced from the kitchen a charming miniature version of the sandwich, and even the reviewer's snotty reference to the "little sandwiches" made famous in the movie *Spinal Tap* did not dampen the moment. Again, cue the music, something befitting the New Orleans' style of sauce, meaning tangy yet sweet, uncomplicated by smokiness, and sure enough, after one enthusiastic expletive, our barbecue snob was reduced to conceding that this was probably the best of its class as well. It was a moment somewhat akin to Ahab finally spotting that whale.

Also locally endorsed, Lisa G's features a different burger each day; the combinations are interesting and the outcome is usually a happy one. Families would probably be comfortable on the deck or in the dining room. While not all of the menu choices are worthy of special music and other fanfare, things have been consistently good. It is the nature of this beast that we cannot eat everything on the menu, but we can assure you we are looking forward to our next visit.

6. Brown Dog Café (Lake Placid, February 2011)

Located on Main Street across from the Hilton, in charming yet touristy Lake Placid village, the Brown Dog Café serves fresh inventive American cuisine, with a premium placed on quality ingredients. It's the kind of place that, as you scan the menu outside the window while scouting the town, you wonder whether the food is either really good, or, as often is the case, is this simply one of those pretentious trendy places that simply exploits upscale tourists.

With about a dozen tables, dinner reservations are mandatory to avoid disappointment, even, as we discovered, on a Sunday night in the off-season. Probably the most sought after tables—and deservingly so—are those at the far end of the dining room that overlook Mirror Lake; overall the restaurant has a quiet, romantic environment, the kind of place with chalkboards, wood beams, and wine racks combining into a pleasant warm ambience. Tables at lunch are far more readily available, and a lighter grill menu features an array of sandwiches that highlight imaginative combinations of ingredients—stuff sure to inspire the home chef. Or, if none of the available options sound sufficiently intriguing, you can build your own sandwich and decide, for example, which type of seven or so breads might go best with the home roasted herbed turkey, and, for embellishments, you might have to scratch your chin when mulling over the implications of cranberry versus roasted tomato chutney.

Our dinner service was professional and welcoming, but certainly not overly intrusive or phony. They've got a good wine list that should please more discerning wine lovers. Additionally, our server expressed confidence in the menu and knowledge about preparation of the dishes—and she did not hesitate to make useful recommendations when asked, proving most helpful. We started with a blended artichoke and carrot soup that made for an unusual palate pleaser. As an appetizer we tried what so many regulars recommend—the smoked duck quesadilla—and found that the "when in Rome" theory worked well. But, perhaps even more to our liking, the filet steak sandwich really delivered; the beef was cooked perfectly—extraordinarily tender—and did not contain even one portion of a slice that was over-cooked or tough. This sandwich is what a steak sandwich should be, not an afterthought made from the cuts left over from Saturday night's prime rib.

For entrees we tried one of the nightly specials, Dover Sole, which came with a mild citrus sauce, and was served over a potato *galette*, a dish that would have made any Parisian bistro proud. Dover sole generally is a delicate fish, easily ruined unless cooked with exactness, and the chef nailed it. In short, while many restaurants try to use "fancy" ingredients in creative ways, it is the chef's palate that separates innovation from a poseur inflicted catastrophe (Food Snob calls this phenomenon the "spinach-garlic ravioli with butterscotch cream sauce" test.)

As a further note, our Food Snob likes to add a "degree of difficulty" to try the staff. So, we explained that we were going to a movie, and our server managed to arrange the timing and order of each dish in such a way that the meal was nicely paced, and we even had ten minutes left over so that we could make the show. Chef Mischa Schaffer made his way to our table, and expressed a genuine interest in making sure we had a good meal, always a nice touch, and further evidence that this is a place truly trying to be excellent.

Given the small size of the venue, and the location, the Brown Dog Café is a little pricier than most of our recommendations—which means their margin for error is lower—and yet most patrons rave about it. Probably not a good dinner option for families, it is best reserved for discerning diners who don't mind paying for quality.

7. Noonmark Diner (Keene Valley, March 2011)

This is the kind of place you go before or after a day of trout fishing in the Ausable River or hiking the many trails throughout the High Peaks. Situated alongside the highway in the village of Keene Valley, the restaurant occupies a lovely spot, sitting in the bottom of a natural bowl surrounded by the "Adirondack Alps." The Noon Mark represents a good destination stop for one of the most scenic drives in the region, Route 73, which has spectacular views as it snakes its way through the valley from the Northway to Lake Placid. The view is bucket-list beautiful on sunny days during the fall foliage season.

The Noon Mark diner is an authentic unpretentious local joint, best known for breakfast and lunch, not dinner. The service is friendly and informal, locals exchange banter and joke with the waitresses, and you feel like you are in a real place. Things do get hectic at times during the seasonal influxes, and you might arrive to find that people are quite content to wait half an hour in line.

The Noon Mark is not a diner in the Jersey sense, no silver trailer, no 24 hour service, no ludicrous number of entrees, no souvlaki or gyros. The Noon Mark separates itself by serving a traditional menu that features a number of homemade, "baked on the premises" items (most marked on the menu with, yep, a smiley face). The prices are so absolutely reasonable that you instantly bond with the place; you're not going to be taken advantage of, and your business is respected. Big city denizens should be positively giddy about the price to quality ratio here.

Stick to those smiley faces as much as possible, we did. When's the last time you had a homemade English muffin ($1.60) with butter and, yes, real strawberry preserves? Fantastic. Food Snob came for the scratch made corned beef hash, cooked crisp, with a sunnyside egg on top ($5.50). The blueberry pancake is not the gigantic fluffy variety, but thin and delicately crisp on the outside, and really, this is a superior version of an Adirondack breakfast staple. Potato choices were good, although, if polled, we preferred the homefries to the fresh cut fries. Oh yeah, almost forgot to mention the fresh homemade bread. The raisin bread, amply loaded with fruit, makes a great choice. One of our reviewers ordered the chicken salad sandwich ($5.00), served on wheat bread; the waitress was almost apologetic about the simplicity; we found it fresh, delicious, creamy with just the right amount of mayonnaise, and utterly fantastic. The sandwich came with an ample bowl of soup; we selected bean and bacon from a list of four; the beans were firm, the broth tasty, the whole thing just another homage to the magic of "simple" cooking.

The pies have attained a high reputation. The raspberry crumble pie lived up to the billing; unfortunately, our one disappointment was that the black raspberry pie did not. So our advice is stick to the crumble pies rather than the traditional ones.

"I am bringing my Dad here," Food Snob announced at the end of the meal, in a rare *Field of Dreams* sort of moment as he wiped crumbs from his face. "We're pretty hapless trout fisherman, but *this* will more than make up for it."

8. Eat-n-Meet Grill (Saranac Lake, April 2011)

In a more perfect existence, every quirky small town would have one "gourmet" take-out place. Naturally, this simple proposition is seldom achieved in the real world. Yet, for the past five years, rumors issuing from Saranac Lake natives continue to boast of the Eat-N-Meet Grill as a "hole-in-the-wall" serving an excellent and interesting cuisine. Our team set off on a dining quest sure to be different from the normal sit-down experience.

Known for its therapeutic fresh air and picturesque views, Saranac Lake is the American *Magic Mountain*, achieving fame in late 19th century as a spa town for consumptives. An appealing array of unique turn-of-the century architecture adds considerably to the appeal—large windows beneath Victorian eaves, historic "cure cottages" wrapped with porches designed for convalescents to take in the air, and numerous brick front stores with plate glass windows—and as you make your way through town, you might find yourself with an incurable desire to explore the interesting small shops that now occupy this unique slice of Americana.

Eat-N-Meet is nestled in just such a setting; you can find it by looking for the life-sized Elvis mannequin hanging out on the second story balcony. The restaurant is small and irresistibly informal, with an open kitchen and just three tables, one a piece of 50's kitsch that adds some comic sensibility to the hard-to-peg aura—is this somehow related to the Elvis upstairs? Framed newspaper articles dot the walls, chiefly about environmentally conscious subjects such as organic cooking and sustainable fish options. Thus, the restaurant's philosophy is manifest; a few other articles cover John Vargo's earlier culinary successes in the Hudson Valley. Tall wooden pantries are lined with an assortment of Chef Vargo's bottled sauces and some other gourmet ingredients ("Aha," exclaimed our dear Food Snob, *"moutarde à la ancienne, just what I needed!"*). Taking advantage of the direct access to the grill, Food Snob asked an endless series of questions about the local ingredients and preparations. Chef John Vargo's answers were complete and enthusiastic; no sign of burnout, the passion here shows. The rest of us hungrily mulled over the selections as F.S. basked in the staff's friendly attention. The menu seems to change daily, and is diligently updated online, a North Country rarity. Savvy locals know to call ahead at least half an hour; this succeeds in both avoiding people like our Food Snob as well as to make sure that the made-to-order food is ready for pick-up. No regular table service exists, but diners are welcome to eat in, and more dining space opens up on the veranda in the summer.

Some menu items are standards. For example, the Reuben sandwich, which merits local legend status, is an ample portion of home-smoked corned beef on a slightly sweet rye bread, with a tangy mix of dressing and sauerkraut. The result is first-rate, sure to satisfy even cranky New Yorkers lamenting their inability to get an authentic deli sandwich "up here." Local spice-aholics are addicted to the Jerk chicken, and a recent effort to tone down the heat nearly provoked widespread demonstrations on the Saranac streets. The menu is incredibly diverse for such a small operation. Tempting regular choices include, among several, pierogies, gyros, locally farmed lamb or beef burgers, pork schnitzels, and kielbasa; more exotic items (some that we missed) include Jamaican curried goat, walleye, Portuguese sardines, and an oyster stew that is evidently superb. A couple of paté dishes are also typically available; provide your own sauterne.

In addition to the Rueben, we tried the baked Alaskan Pollack tacos, served in blue corn tortillas, with salsa verde, sour cream, and ample fixings on the side; well-seasoned, the ensemble proved tasty. The *coq au vin*, consisted of chicken pieces, mushrooms and onions, served over basmati rice. It came out succulent and, though lightly sauced, had ample flavor from the use of fresh herbs. We couldn't resist having an order of hush puppies (for a dollar) that conjured up the tastes of the South. The coleslaw was also good, if you like the vinegary-pepper variety. Overall, the food's quality left us regretting that we couldn't sample all the intriguing menu options—no doubt the French have a phrase for this particular kind of longing.

Finally, some tips on the Eat-N-Meet grill. Credit cards are not accepted, although an ATM exists on-site. No alcohol is served. Without servers and by keeping physical overhead low, the prices are so incredibly reasonable that it seems like they should be kept a secret. The portions are generally large, making it even more of a find. If foodie heaven exists—a sort of Valhalla where feats of culinary arts are celebrated in song, and where innovative chefs like John Vargo are escorted upward to the sky by former waitresses turned Valkyries—places like the Eat-n-Meet Grill maybe ubiquitous. But here in the Adirondacks, we count our blessings.

9. Lakeview Deli (Saranac Lake, May 2011)

Thanks in part to road conditions after the historic Adirondack flood of 2011, we got to the door of the Lakeview Deli about five minutes after closing. Peering in just out of curiosity to see what we had missed, we suddenly found ourselves being cheerily waved inside by the owner of this family run favorite, who was also intently making fresh baked goods behind the counter. Of the three people working, not one micro-gesture of frustration or impatience could be detected; instead, we encountered incredible friendliness and, to our many questions, helpful responses. This sort of service deserves pointing out, and speaks highly of the morale of the Lakeview Deli team—and sure, in this case, they actually did have us at hello.

We can report that the sandwiches, much praised by Saranac folks, not only lived up to billing, but also would have earned a good review even if the service had been surly. In addition to serving Boar's Head meats, the Deli takes the time to roast their own fresh turkey and pork, and that's a difference maker. If you are the kind of person who can't wait for the sandwiches the day after Thanksgiving, then the "Fresh Roast" turkey sandwich is a must. Food Snob contentedly devoured his sandwich, even sprinkling a little salt on it, something, he pointed out, that really brings out fresh roasted meat. Going on a local tip, we also tried the Fresh Mozzarella sandwich—a toasted sub with pesto mayonnaise, lettuce, tomato and onion—that proved to be tender in texture (heavenly, pronounced Food Snob) with magnificent flavor. Certainly this had to be one of the best vegetarian items we'd had over the course of our dining Odyssey. The macaroni salad succeeded in not being too heavy on the mayonnaise, and the other salad options—potato, tuna-macaroni, and coleslaw—looked highly acceptable.

While some folks say it's pricey, it can't be more than a dollar or so more than any of the less than mediocre sub chains. The extra quality is a steal. If you're going boating or sightseeing, enhance your experience by taking a picnic lunch from here.

10. Simply Gourmet Deli (Lake Placid, April 2011)

The Simply Gourmet Deli has two locations now in Lake Placid; we ate at the original (yellow) house on the outskirts of town on Saranac Avenue. The other location is on Main Street, next to the library, but is called Big Mountain Deli and *Crêperie*. The downside to the more convenient location is that you can't get the "to die for" crêpes. However, the upside is easier parking during peak downtown hours, and a larger selection of specialty foods.

The menu features 46 sandwiches, each named for one of the High Peaks in the Adirondacks, a successful gimmick partly derived from the celebrity deli kick, except that instead of the "Cary Grant" you can order the "Mount Algonquin." Like a big city deli, lunch time can get pretty hectic. Some people find the ordering process amusing; others find it frustrating. Patrons write their order onto a small slip of duplicating paper, circling the number of the sandwich, and indicating the type of bread, along with any sides requested. Submit the copy to the counter, and wait until your name is called. While Seinfeld fans might have a momentary flashback to the "Soup Nazi" episode, we can assure you that you won't be banned or yelled at if you get the paperwork wrong. And, whatever the odd sensation that somehow this deli has taken its slice of bureaucracy too far—we assure you on a busy day that you'll appreciate the friendly efficiency.

The sandwiches are generally good to great, featuring Boar's Head meats and a choice from five fresh breads. We stuck with the numbered sandwiches rather than "create our own." Food Snob enjoyed #25, the Mount Marshal, certain that the rest of us would not know what *sopressata* was and figured he could get away without sharing his sandwich. The #2 Algonguin—roast turkey, applewood smoked bacon, avocado, sprouts, and Russian dressing—ranked even better.

Insiders like the homemade brownies and giant cookies rate highly, and there is a nice selection of salads. Eminently accommodating to its customers needs, the Simply Gourmet Deli also offers Gluten free, dairy free, vegetarian and vegan options. Locals also strongly endorse the breakfast, featuring paninnis, bagels, flapjacks, burritos and various granola cereals, all reasonable priced.

11. The Cottage (Lake Placid, August 2010)

Whether you want to relax after a tiring afternoon on the slopes or need a break from shopping, the Cottage, on Main Street, is Lake Placid's most charming watering hole. Sitting on the edge of Mirror Lake, the Cottage has a striking view of the mountains in the distance (and, inside, a poster labels all of the peaks for you). Casual but, respect the house rule against cell phones to enjoy the full charm of this venue, where a mix of seasonal and year-round residents mingle with skiers, Olympians, and tourists; personality types run from the haughty and pretentious (yes, so Food Snob has someone to talk to) to the affable and low-key.

The friendly staff keeps the mood light and the drinks flowing. The Cottage has daily wine, beer and drink specials, but we often indulge in one of the infamous Bloody Marys, served in a Mason Jar. Most nights, Bridgette, the winner of the "Best Bartender in the Tri-Lakes Area" for two years running, will take care of you.

The menu at the Cottage features paninis, wraps, and vegetarian specials; it's a small kitchen, but has a decent variety of choices. We enjoyed "Lisa's Favorite," a hot open-faced roast beef sandwich, with sautéed onions, mushrooms, melted brie and horseradish mayonnaise. Locals of the vegetarian persuasion suggest the Stuffed Avocado with crab meat salad. Regulars salute the signature "Drunken Kraut" or the "Really Drunken Kraut"—no, these are not pejorative terms for members of the German Bobsled team—but rather jumbo black angus frankfurters steamed in local beer and topped off with sauerkraut. The Really Drunken Kraut is more decadent with cheddar jack cheese, chili, and sauerkraut.

Like many year-round venues here, the Cottage adjusts for the season. In the summer, enjoy the breeze from the deck or venture out for a stroll on the dock; on Sundays catch the live music on the deck. During the fall, the fire pit and heat lamps counter the chill of the salubrious Adirondack air, and an autumn moon over the lake can makes for a fine setting. In the winter, patrons enjoy warming up by the woodstove, or watching ice skaters or the broom ball tournaments.

Be sure not to miss some of the atmosphere inside. Start with the super cool trap door under the bartender's feet, savor the chic martini glasses, and trade barbs with the wait staff and bartenders. The Cottage rates as one of our favorite places to hang out in Lake Placid.

12. Jimmy's 21 (Lake Placid, January 2011)

Run by Bosnians who left the Balkans to start a business in America, Jimmy's 21 serves Italian food. On Main Street, Jimmy's has a great view of Mirror Lake, with three levels to the restaurant and two outdoor decks. A table by the window greatly enhances the experience of dining here. Budget conscious regulars swear by the early bird special from 4-6.

Locals come here for a few dishes mainly. First off, ask for the fresh pasta; it's not automatically served, and is worth specifying. If you're not in the mood for red sauce, try the clams in white sauce over linguine. Loaded with pieces of clams in a hearty portion, the sauce succeeds in not being too garlicky or rich. The fettuccine *carbonara* makes a popular choice, while others endorse the veal or chicken *parmigiana*. One of our good friends swears by the steak sandwich and fries (for $11.95) at the bar. The only real disappointment was the broiled seafood platter, which Food Snob found six fathoms deep in excess butter.

Service here can be great, but, in peak season, the staff can be harried and indifferent. Like many Adirondack restaurants, consistency can be a problem. Dining in January on a busy Saturday (we were staying at The Haus just down the street, great spot, and really one of the coolest and most affordable accommodations in Placid), we had a good experience, and found the prices reasonable.

13. Lake Placid Pub & Brewery (Lake Placid, May 2011)

The most popular local microbrew is Ubu, born here at the Lake Placid Pub and Brew, where it is still made to its original specifications for local consumption. A ruby red English Ale, this malty beer has garnered an incredibly devoted following who appreciate the "nutty flavor" and "dark cherry" undertones. The

FX Matt Brewing Company in Utica has since taken over wider production and distribution. However, purists feel there has been a slight drop off in the quality, and insist on coming to the Pub for the "real thing" which has just a tad more "sweetness."

Finding the place is a bit tricky, as the Pub is just off Main Street, past the Mirror Lake beach and across from the tennis courts. With a bar and tables on two levels, and it's a good place to take in a game. The upstairs has a large collection of college pennants hanging from the walls, and we watched the Kentucky Derby at the bar to a packed house; downstairs, the original bar known as PJ O'Neill's has dark wood and a quieter atmosphere. At either place, get a seat at the bar to socialize. If you're not completely sold on the Ubu, try the beer sampler, where you can taste six different four-ounce offerings before deciding on your favorite. Lake Placid I.P.A. and 46er Pale Ale are also popular choices, and the rotating seasonal brews can be interesting.

The pub fare is reasonably priced, fans endorse the hamburgers, and, to a lesser extent, the barbecue. Insiders gush that it is the "best pub fare around" with things like "proper nachos" and even some vegetarian selections. We liked the bangers and mash as well as the Welsh Rarebit, and the French onion soup, made with Ubu, is terrific. For dessert, the S'Mores are a lot of fun.

14. The Belvedere (Saranac Lake, May 2011)

The Belvedere, serving since 1933, is one of those dark knotty pine Adirondack retro places largely unchanged in the last 50 years. The food's about the same, the staff are often direct descendants of the founders, and the décor and furniture is just how you remember it, maybe with a piece of duct tape on the bottom of the chair to hold things together just a little bit longer. Baby boomers will be overcome with the thick sauce of nostalgia, half-expecting some long lost uncle to come sauntering in, looking as he once did, calling the bartender "doll" while ordering his Manhattan. Younger diners, especially fans of the television series *Madmen,* can feel what it was like on those boozy sixties weekends, when guys like Don Draper stopped in on their way north from the city for some fresh air, all the while dangling cigarettes in an endless chain-smoking marathon meant to help them unwind.

Cocktail prices have remained in line with the setting, as $7.50 bought two well drinks. Check out the old refrigerator still humming in the background, or play some tunes on the juke box. Locals don't wax poetic about the food, but somehow find themselves drawn here for the steaks or the broiled seafood anyway; others like the chicken *parmigiana.* The blue cheese dressing gets accorded some superlatives ("best in the mountains"). For real retro authenticity, get a side of cottage cheese, and, for something different, try the anchovies in olive oil.

The Adirondacks in 60s and 70s once were a beacon of now-defunct theme parks and assorted other tourist traps. Gaslight Village in Lake George once celebrated the early twentieth century, Frontier Town the Wild West. Those places have long since been boarded up or demolished, and boomers have been cut off from this oddly resonant by-gone world. Interestingly, a place like the Belvedere is, in its way, a theme park of its own, a taste of an era many people never dreamed they'd be sentimental to experience again.

15. Pan Dolce (Lake Placid, June 2011)

From the outside, and even on the inside, this new Lake Placid venue has the appearance of a chain—in part because the premises were converted from a Burger King. Indeed, the owner is considering Pan Dolce—a name meaning sweet bread/cake/dessert in Italian—as a prototype. But for now, the fate of this putative empire is in the hands of Chef Chris McDermott, who worked previously at the Longview and the Adirondack Hotel in Long Lake where we became familiar with his work, and who now has the opportunity to raise his game in this executive opportunity.

The interior of the restaurant, with warm red and yellow colors, seemed vaguely reminiscent of a Panera Bread—this perception received further reinforcement when the focaccia/bread arrived. At the time of our visit, the restaurant clearly was undergoing its shakedown cruise, with first time wait staff and a dinner menu limited to only three specials beyond the sandwich menu. We chose an interesting take on the standard "surf and turf" which consisted of a spicy marinated flank steak and lobster ravioli in a passion fruit sauce, which came in a very colorful attractive presentation. The steak was tender, cooked to specification, and had a nice bit of heat. The lobster ravioli, unfortunately, was too subtle for the passion fruit flavors, though the sauce worked well to balance against the spiciness of the beef. Naturally Food Snob shared his observations with the chef, who seemed to take the advice in stride. Overall, despite the tactical error, the dish succeeded.

Given the Pan Dolce name, it's probably not a surprise that the desserts tasted superb. The blueberry lemonade cake made a strong case for best dessert of the tour, tart, moist, with icing that warranted entry into confectionery heaven. Food Snob, waxing about his days in Vienna and Prague, was duly impressed with the Linzer Torte. A vanilla bean cupcake, taken to go, became a sublime midnight snack; a must purchase for vanilla enthusiasts. The coffee is also recommended, a clear step up from the afterthought that the beverage represents in many establishments.

Overall, we promise to come back next year to give readers a full report as this operation gets its first year underway, until then we are cautiously optimistic. Meanwhile, don't miss the desserts, or stop by in the morning for freshly made New York style (chewy) bagels.

16. Red Fox (Saranac Lake, April 2011)

The Adirondacks have a number of restaurants that fulfill the market for traditional fare and big portions, generally drawing an older crowd on Friday and Saturday evenings; you can spot these places by the number of large cars in the parking lot. While Food Snob cannot comprehend this nostalgic craving for the cuisine of the late seventies, none-the-less, it is an Adirondack thing. So, yes, the Red Fox is that kind of place, selected here because, all in all, its portions are larger and its prices pretty reasonable. So if you're in the mood for a prime rib, salad, and baked potato, this is a fine venue to have it. If you're looking for risky or innovative dishes, this is not the place, unless you consider "surf and turf" cutting edge.

You might want to start off with a Bloody Mary; the tomato juice is featured anyway so why not enhance it. Meals include soup, salad, and the entrée. The loaf of bread comes out hot and crisp, very good, and unwrapping the tinfoil from the butter reinforces the 70s thing. Pay the extra for the French onion soup; beefy, it succeeds by not being overpoweringly salty; the chicken noodle, on the other hand, was a tad thin and weak. The homemade Italian dressing is good; it deserved a better selection of produce, so we ended up dipping our bread into it. The prime rib was tender and served with ample *au jus*, but you'll have to ask for the horseradish. The lamb chops represented the largest such portion we had ever seen, nine pieces, tender and seasoned with rosemary, served with mint jelly. Locals recommend the chicken *parmigiana* and the shrimp scampi.

We recommend that you try to sit in the front dining room; the back one can seem cavernous and eerily quiet. Adirondack photographs and paintings of red foxes dominate the décor. None of the desserts are homemade, so we passed.

NORTHERN ADIRONDACK LOCAL LOWDOWN

Elizabethtown

Arsenal Inn & Motel
7581 Court Street
Elizabethtown, NY 12932
(518) 873-6863

Local Lowdown: "Excellent food and staff".... Family run....
"Good" .... "an A+."

Keene/Keene Valley

Noonmark Diner
1770 NYS Route 73
Keene Valley, NY 12943
(518) 576-4499
www.noonmarkdiner.com

Local Lowdown: "Great pies and homemade desserts" ....
Traditional family pit-stop to eat.... "Homemade English
muffins are a must!".... 20-25 pies and baked goods on menu at
anytime.... "You have to get the Raspberry Cheese Crumb Pie."

Baxter Mountain Tavern
10050 NYS Route 9N
Keene, NY 12942
(518) 576-9990
www.baxtermountaintavern.com

Local Lowdown: Standard grill fare.... "Beautiful views" from the back dining room.

Lake Placid

Ashley's Café
2726 Main Street # 1
Lake Placid, NY 12946
(518) 523-2540

Local Lowdown: Good local coffee house.... "Yummy" .... Breakfasts, very popular.... Good pancakes, banana oatmeal.

The Boathouse
654 Mirror Lake Drive
Lake Placid, New York 12946
(518) 523-4822

Local Lowdown: Great view on water.... "Go here for the sunset view" .... Known for different drinks.... "Food can be inconsistent, so enjoy the bar."

The Brown Dog Café

2409 Main Street
Lake Placid, NY 12946
(518) 523-3036
www.4peaks.com/fawbdog.htm

Local Lowdown: Gourmet sandwiches and wine bar.... "Great for lunch!" .... A "little pricey, but good," recommended for "people from the city." Wine pairings.... Over 60 wines served by the glass! .... "Nice balcony seating, better for couples" .... Reservations for dinner are requested.

Caffé Rustica

1936 Saranac Avenue
Lake Placid, NY 12946
(518) 523-7511
http://cafferustica.com

Local Lowdown: Rustic Italian and Mediterranean food.... Serves lunch and dinner.... Quaint.... Just expanded.... "Amazing food—never a bad meal" .... In the Price Chopper mini-mall.... "Pricey" .... "Not good for kids." Walk-in only, gourmet pizza, pasta, "nice wines."

Caribbean Cowboy

2126 Saranac Avenue
Lake Placid NY 12946
(518) 523-3836

Local Lowdown: "Hole in the wall" behind the Saranac Sourdough sandwich shop.... "Awesome, different food," especially if you like funky sauces and combinations.

Cascade Inn
Cascade Road, Route 73
Lake Placid, NY 12946
(518) 523-2130
www.cascadeinn.com

Local Lowdown: Cozy-old school restaurant a little out of town.... Serves soup and salad with dinner.... Known for steaks/Delmonico.... Mom & Pop restaurant.... "Down to Earth" .... "Fun" .... "Full moon parties" during winter. Dinner reservations recommended.

Chair Six
5992 Sentinel Road
Lake Placid, NY 12946
(518) 523-3630
http://chair6.com

Local Lowdown: Fresh baked bread and pastries.... "Great breakfasts" .... Wednesday night set menu for $20-$25!

The Cottage
77 Mirror Lake Drive
Lake Placid NY 12946
(518) 523-2544
www.mirrorlakeinn.com/dining-cottage.cfm

Local Lowdown: "Cozy place right on Mirror Lake" .... Known for their pub-style foods and salads.... Mixed berry flan and key lime pie are "delicious" .... "Incredible views" of the high peaks and Mirror Lake.... "Best outdoor seating in Placid."

The Dancing Bears Lounge

2384 Saranac Avenue
Lake Placid, NY 12946-1105
(518) 523-4411
www.highpeaksresort.com/dining/dancing-bears

Local Lowdown: "Good lobster roll" .... "Interesting crowd, great for people watching" .... "Gorgeous" view of the peaks from 2nd floor.... "The upscale terrace is a must in summer!" Great for breakfast and burgers, pizzas, and nachos.... Fondue dishes, fire pit outside, upstairs tiki torches, fleece blankets provided for colder nights.

Desperado's

2090 Saranac Avenue
Lake Placid NY 12946
(518) 523-1507
www.desperadosrestaurant.com

Local Lowdown: Huge tequila selection.... "Local place."

Downhill Grill

6143 Sentinel Road
Lake Placid, NY 12946
(518) 523-9510
www.menumart.com/downhillgrill/index.htm

Local Lowdown: Cool bar—food pub-style.... "Good parking and soup" .... "The perfect spot for Iron Man Day."

Hohmeyer's Lake Clear Lodge

6319 State Route 30
Lake Clear, NY 12945
(518) 891-1489
www.adirodackalps.com

Local Lowdown: "Beautiful and good food" .... Over 300 Old World beers and over 350 boutique wines.... 1886 hand-hewn dining room.... "Upscale, nice."

Interlaken Inn

39 Interlaken Avenue
Lake Placid NY 12946
(518) 523-3180
www.theinterlakeninn.com

Local Lowdown: "Richard's"—the Interlaken Inn Restaurant.... Country inn/pub setting.... Very elegant.... Excellent wines.... "Must try the Crab Cake and Venison" .... New chef, so things may be different. Reservations recommended.... Will review in 2012 edition.

Jimmy 21's

Top 46

2425 Main Street
Lake Placid, NY 12946
(518) 523-2353

Local Lowdown: Conventional Italian restaurant.... Great view.... On Mirror Lake across from the movie theatre.... Known for their steaks, Italian dishes and seafood.... "Sit at the bar and get the steak and fries, $11.95" .... Regulars recommend the Mozzarella in Carozza and Fettuccine Carbonara.... Great fries!

Kanu at the Whiteface Lodge

7 Whiteface Inn Lane
Lake Placid, NY 12946
(518) 523-0510
www.thewhitefacelodge.com/food_wine

Local Lowdown: Very family oriented.... "Request a table on
the side" .... Elegant.... Tapas and two size entrees available....
"Good wines."

Lake Placid Lodge

144 Lodge Way
Lake Placid, NY 12946
www.lakeplacidlodge.com/Dining/Dining-Reservations

Local Lowdown: "Not to be missed" .... Good to go by boat....
Very high-end (but jacket not necessary).... Two venues: Maggie's
Pub or Artisans Restaurant, both have tables inside or outside....
Dinner starts at $70/person with tasting menus up to $125.
"Fancy and romantic" .... "Farm to table" .... Children 12 and
above are welcome.... Reservation recommended.

Lake Placid Pub & Brewery

813 Main Street
Lake Placid NY 12946
(518) 523-3813
www.ubuale.com

Local Lowdown: Good novelty place.... "Sweet bar food" ....
Always a great time.... Reasonable prices.... "Awesome beer" ....
"Beer first, food second."

Lisa G's

6125 Sentinel Road
Lake Placid, NY 12946-3508
(518) 523-2093
www.lisags.com

Local Lowdown: Off the main drag in Lake Placid on your
way to the ski jumps.... Known for their wings, burgers, and
margaritas" .... "Best Wings ever!" .... Belly up to the bar and get
a Jam Jar, good whiskey drink served in Mason jar.... Nice back
deck with waterfall.... "I love Lisa G's!"

Liquids and Solids at the Handlebar

6115 Sentinel Road
Lake Placid, NY 12946
(518) 837-5012

Local Lowdown: Across from Lisa G's off the main drag, on your
way to the ski jumps.... Wait staff from other restaurants often
recommend this place! .... Trendy, fun.... "Good beer selection
and funky mixed drinks" .... Small and large plates.... "Great
drinks, beers, and wine list."

Mirror Lake Inn

77 Mirror Lake Drive
Lake Placid NY 12946
(518) 302-3000
www.mirrorlakeinn.com/dining.cfm

Local Lowdown: Beautiful dining rooms/views, has a very
romantic feel.... "Expensive" .... "Formal dining room for an older
crowd with perhaps the best service in Lake Placid" .... Award
of Excellence four years running.... "Celebrity sightings" ....
Reservations recommended.

Nicolas on Main Street

2517 Main Street
Lake Placid, NY 12946
(518) 523-5853
www.nicolasandgrill211.com

Local Lowdown: Mediterranean-style cuisine.... Wood-fired pizza.... Large eatery across from the Olympic Center.... "Upscale setting with a beautiful bar."

Northwoods Inn

2520 Main Street
Lake Placid, NY 12946-3498
(518) 523-1818
(800) 294-7171
www.northwoodsinn.com/dining.asp

Local Lowdown: Hotel on the main street of Lake Placid with three different dining venues.... "The Cabin"—bar atmosphere; nice at night.... "Northern Exposure"—lunch and dinner with Wednesday night specials.... "The Pavilion"—breakfast.... "Fun to sit out on the sidewalk" .... "Good service."

Pan Dolce

Top 46

2166 Saranac Avenue
Lake Placid, NY 12946
(518) 302-5005
(800) 294-7171
http://pandolcelakeplacid.com

Local Lowdown: Brand new restaurant with coffee shop serving breakfast and lunch.... "Small dinner menu—but so far so good".... Just opened this past March.... "Good New York style bagels".... "Unbelievable" cakes/pastries! "Catch dessert here" if you get nothing else.

Paradox Lodge

2169 Saranac Avenue
Lake Placid, NY 12946
(518) 523-9078
(877) 743-9078
www.paradoxlodge.com/restaurant.html

Local Lowdown: "Best turkey melt ever!" .... Good food, sausage.... Very exclusive, need reservations.... "Expensive" .... "Owner's a real character" .... Previously owner of the Steak & Stinger.

Rumors

Main Street
Lake Placid, NY 12946

Local Lowdown: Adirondack night club.... Dancing.... Don't go before 11pm—it'll be empty.... Can almost always find a good time here.... Friendly bartenders.... Mostly a younger crowd.

Simply Gourmet:
BIG Mountain Deli & Crêperie

1983 Saranac Avenue
Lake Placid, NY 12946
(518) 523-3111
(518)523-3222
www.simplygourmetlakeplacid.com

Local Lowdown: Sandwiches named after 46 high peaks....
"Lattés good too!" .... Two locations: "Simply Gourmet"
on Saranac Avenue, near the Price Chopper Mall, or "Big
Mountain Deli & Crêperie" next to the library on Main Street....
"Great" cheese selections & desserts.... Awesome "build-your-
own sandwich" selections.... Can call or fax in your order
ahead.... So many choices, so little time.... "Fantastic!"

Soul Shine Bagel
128 Main Street
Lake Placid, NY 12946
(518) 523-9772

Local Lowdown: Bagels and snacks.... "Great" coffee.... Quick
place to get something to eat on the main drag.

Steak & Seafood Company

2442 Main Street
Lake Placid, NY 12946
(518) 523-1629
www.greatadirondacksteakandseafood.com
www.adirondackbrewing.com

Local Lowdown: Family steak house with a conventional menu....
Across from "The Haus" and next to the movie theater.... Serves
lunch and dinner (breakfast on weekends and holidays)..... "Good
soups".... "Beer is better than Lake Placid Brewery, not as dark and
hoppy".... "Great outdoor seating".... Nice folks who run it.... Good
Early Bird Special.... "Servers can be overwhelmed at times."

Veranda Restaurant

1 Olympic Drive
Lake Placid, NY 12946-1423
(518) 523-3339

Local Lowdown: Traditional French menu.... "Killer view from
outside seating, go there around sunset!" .... "Good food and
service" .... "Romantic place."

Villa Vespa

47 Saranac Avenue
Lake Placid, NY 12946
(518) 523-9789
www.villavespa.net

Local Lowdown: "Back parking lot seating" .... "Decent" take
out food—awesome garlic bread.... "It's alright."

Wise Guys
11 School Street
Lake Placid, NY 12946-1423
(518) 523-4446
www.wiseguyslp.com

Local Lowdown: Happy Hour 3:30 - 7pm.... Huge deck.... Good bands.... Serves late-night food!

Zig Zags
134 Main Street
Lake Placid, NY 12946
(518) 523-8221

Local Lowdown: Good bar/bands.... Local hole in the wall.... Darts/pool.... "Lots of famous bobsledders go there" .... Fun on weekends.... "Whatever you do, don't sit in the bobsled" .... Good times.

Paul Smiths

St. Regis Restaurant
Route 86
Paul Smiths, NY 12970
(518) 327-9437

Local Lowdown: Restaurant run by the Hotel and Restaurant Management students at Paul Smith's College.... "Inexpensive, yet good meals with formal service" .... The café overlooks beautiful St. Regis Lake.... "No liquor, but very good food!" .... "Features creative menu."

Port Henry

George's Restaurant
16 Broad Street
Port Henry, NY 12974
(518) 546-3026

Local Lowdown: "Go for George's Special Three Meatball Appetizer" .... "Good French Dip."

Saranac

Big Daddy's Family Restaurant
4655 County Road 3
Saranac, NY 12981
(518) 293-7666

Local Lowdown: Good for breakfast.... Fried food/traditional food.... Good portions.

Jingles Country Cooking
3357 County Road 3
Saranac, NY 12981
(518) 293-8272

Local Lowdown: Located what seems to some— "in the middle of nowhere" on your way to Plattsburgh on Route 3.... Pancake contest.... "Huge, delicious" pancakes.... If you can eat three pancakes, they'll give you a T-shirt! Good (tiny) diner!

Saranac Lake

Belvedere

102 Bloomingdale Avenue
Saranac Lake, NY 12983
(518) 891-9873

Local Lowdown: "Good Mom & Pop place" .... Third generation Italian/Continental restaurant that opened in 1933.... Also known for their steaks and generous portions.... "Best homemade blue cheese in the North Country" .... Fun bar with pool table.

Blue Moon Café

55 Main Street
Saranac Lake, NY 12983
(518) 891-1310
www.bluemooncafe-adk.com

Local Lowdown: Serving breakfast, lunch, and dinner.... "Great coffee and breakfast" .... Homemade corned-beef hash, soups and stews.... Diverse cheese menu.... Wine pairings.... "Good wine list."

Casa Del Sol

154 Lake Flower Avenue
Saranac Lake, NY 12983-2464
(518) 891-0977
www.casadelsolsaranaclake.com

Local Lowdown: "Best Mexican food in the area" .... "Great selection and filling—you won't go home hungry!" .... "Confusing hours, call in advance" .... "Usually good, but sadly inconsistent."

Charlie's Inn

43 Junction Road
Lake Clear, NY 12945
(518) 891-9858
www.charliesinn.tripod.com/index.html

Local Lowdown: Good stop for snowmobilers to stop and warm up! .... Near Adirondack Airport.... Fun place.

DJ's Rustic Restaurant

151 Broadway
Saranac Lake, NY 12983
(518) 891-9735

Local Lowdown: "Really cheap and rustic" .... "Our waitress was mean (but in a fun way)" .... "Good food, hole in the wall" .... "Diner dive."

Donnelly's Ice Cream

1556 State Route 86
Saranac Lake, NY 12983
(518) 891-1404

Local Lowdown: One flavor a day homemade soft ice cream.... "Best ice cream for hundreds of miles" .... Nice view.... "Best ice cream in the Adirondacks" .... Amazing view of Whiteface.... Be careful or "you may get hit by a car as drivers often careen recklessly into the lot, desperate for a taste of the best ice cream ever!" .... "Eat quick if it's hot—the cones will topple!"

Eat 'N Meet Grill and Larder

Top 46

139 Broadway
Saranac Lake, NY 12983
(518) 891-3149
www.eatnmeet.com

Local Lowdown: "Funky, different themes" .... Menu changes daily.... "It does take a while to get food" .... A big Elvis mannequin on the porch.... Can play mini-golf while you wait.... No credit cards.

Gaga's

2 State Street
Bloomingdale, NY 12913
(518) 891-8024

Local Lowdown: Good stop for snowmobilers.... Off Route 3, near Saranac.

La Bella

564 Lake Flower Avenue
Saranac Lake, NY 12983-2464
(518) 891-1551

Local Lowdown: A good local, Italian place.... "Good bread served with a spicy dip" .... "Friendly staff and decent Italian-American style food (especially the pastas)."

Lake View Deli

Top 46

102 River Street
Saranac Lake, NY 12983
(518) 891-2101
www.lakeviewdeli.com

Local Lowdown: Excellent sandwiches.... "Best salami/ mozzarella sandwich" .... They do catering too! .... "Best deli around!" .... "Worth the wait" .... "Awesome deli!"

Left Bank Café

36 Broadway
Saranac Lake, NY 12983
(518) 354-8166

Local Lowdown: French bistro—opened last year.... "Really good" food.... Coffee/tea shop.... Dog-friendly.... To be reviewed 2012.

Little Italy

27 Main Street
Saranac Lake, NY 12983-2464
(518) 891-9000

Local Lowdown: Good, consistent American-Italian food.... "Ask if toppings are fresh or canned before ordering pizza."

Nona Fina

151 River Street
Saranac Lake, NY 12983-2464
(518) 891-4444

Local Lowdown: Mixed reviews, some people say it depends on your waiter.... "Good bread and friendly people" .... "Solid Italian cuisine; relaxed and friendly."

Red Fox

5034 State Street
Saranac Lake, NY 12983
(518) 891-2127

Local Lowdown: Known for their steaks and lamb being "very good" .... Choice of soup or juice.... "Decent price wise—generous portions" .... Also known for their prime rib and chicken *parmigiana*.

The Shamrock

83 County Route 55
Saranac Lake, NY 12983
(518) 891-6180

Local Lowdown: Outside of Saranac Lake going towards Paul Smiths.... "In Gabriels or Brighton on Split Rock Road" .... Good burgers and great for snowmobilers, on snowmobile trail.... "Looks like a little house—don't miss it."

Willsboro

Turtle Island Café
3790 Main Street
Willsboro, NY 12996
(518) 963-7417
www.turtleislandcafe.com

Local Lowdown: The fish and seafood purchased is only wild caught and of sustainable species.... "Dave Martin, chef, (graduate of the Culinary Institute of America with over twenty years experience).... used to be at Hungry Trout" .... Fresh ingredients from local places.... "Very good" .... To be reviewed in 2012.

Wilmington

Hungry Trout Restaurant & Inn
5239 NYS Route 86
Wilmington, NY 12997
(518) 946-2217
www.hungrytrout.com

Local Lowdown: One mile North of Whiteface Mountain—fifteen minute drive from Lake Placid.... Beautiful scenery.... Waterfall/brook.... Bands on the weekends—great after the mountain during the winter but good during the summer too! .... Can eat downstairs at "R.F. McDougall's Pub" too.... Ability to order off both the pub menu or the upstairs dining menu.... Trout, quail, venison, steak.... Has "fallen off dramatically" from lofty ratings of previous years.

Steinhoff's Sportsman's Inn

Route 86
PO Box 426
Wilmington, NY
(518)946-2220
www.steinhoffssportsmansinn.com

Local Lowdown: "Great" meatball sandwich.... Cozy
Adirondack restaurant.

Wilderness Inn II Restaurant

5481 Route 86
Wilmington, NY
(518) 946-2391
www.wildernessinnadk.com / WildernessRestaurant.html

Local Lowdown: A local hangout.... "Good stuffed pork chop."

Adirondack Eats

SOUTH/EAST REGION:

Lake George

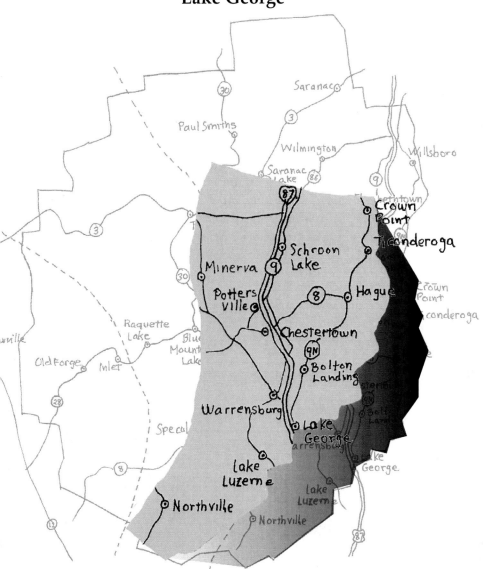

1. Farmhouse at the Top of the World (Lake George, June 2011)

About five miles out of town on the eastern shore, the Farmhouse at the Top of the World ranks as the best restaurant in the Lake George area. While locals consider it expensive, a host of lesser lights on the Village strip can set you back pretty good, all without serving anything comparable in quality or imagination. Hearty appetites may feel that the price here is too high for the portions, while some other folks may be in the mood for a more traditional menu. However, for foodie couples traveling in the region, we'd consider it an absolute must—stop meal.

As we made our way up the mountainside road toward the golf course, we felt a certain inner lightness as we ascended beyond the honking horns and carnival atmosphere below. A peaceful, quiet, and contemplative environment proved to be a perfect fit for the food to come. The fairways of the golf course actually make for a wide and stunning vista of the surrounding mountain region—a table here during leaf season would represent a celestial experience. The restaurant looks to be a farmhouse on the outside—surrounded by enough flowers that you seem to be stepping into a Mary Cassatt painting. On the inside, it is also a functioning country club, but far more "Adirondack Camp" in feel, due to the old knotty pine interior, than something *Caddyshack*.

The four window tables are suitably romantic; book one of these if possible. Beer lovers will be pleased to choose from an interesting selection of bottles, including such favorites as Brooklyn Lager, Smuttynose Porter, and Troeg's Hopback Lager. The wine list is available by the glass, and each wine is given a pithy and creative description—such as "full-bodied and velvety with flavors of plum and woodland berries"—sure to help with pairings. An adventurous or well-travelled palate is probably a requisite for the ideal Farmhouse patron. Unusual ingredients abound. Don't worry, however, if you don't know what argyle yogurt, gribiche, toma celena (thought it was a town in Arizona), and fideus are, you'll find the wait staff helpful and informative. Sure, we were afraid to ask what "komatsuna" means; Food Snob even turned a little red at the sound of it (okay, it's basically an Asian turnip, and it requires no particular physical flexibility to eat). Yes, the menu is designed for conversation.

This may be heaven for the organic foodie hedonist. Vegetarians will find numerous creative choices such as handmade tortellini with New York cheeses and asparagus, and, if vegans represent a Lost Generation to many chefs, they will find something delectable here from the simple snack menu or by special request. The tasting menu is the way to go for most first time diners, although everyone at the table must join in on it. The leisurely-paced five course meal is set at $55 dollars per person—selected wine pairings can be added for another $25. What follows is a fascinating dining *experience* that allows Chef Kevin London a creative opportunity to showcase his talents. Diners inform the server as to their likes, and dislikes; other than that, it's up to the chef to impress you.

Our tasting menu started with a single fried oyster (cornmeal) and a crisp fried pork skin, served with a drizzle of cocktail sauce— the ensemble, if tough to hold together, certainly enhanced each element beautifully. The second course, grilled asparagus and ham with "this morning's egg" played to the Farmhouse idea; it came drizzled with saba and served on a piece of slate. At this point, we felt like we spotted trend here, that a few fresh ingredients confidently served with relatively simple presentations would be the theme. Truly fresh eggs, skillfully grilled asparagus, a delicious local ham, well, what's not to like? Then the third course came, not only smashing the trend, but representing, according to Food Snob, probably the finest dish we had in the course of doing the book. A grilled lamb chop served over a long-simmered lamb ragout, all with a savory yet tart sauce made from N.Y. cheese curd, cumin, and lamb stock—well, we're talking Michelin star superb. The fourth course—cod, mussels and clams served over a grilled crouton with a green sauce broth—ranked as very, very good, but not transcendent like the lamb. Lastly, dessert, a French-style chocolate *pot de crème*, with two fresh strawberries, and a dark chocolate fried wafer, closed the meal perfectly.

It wasn't until we made our way a back down the mountain that we caught sight of the vistas of Lake George in the sunset. With the blue water deepening in the long shadows of the mountains, and garnished with an evening mist, the stunning aesthetic moment seemed as if it had been planned—like some other-worldly sixth course paired by nature—to complete our magnificent meal.

2. The Grist Mill (Warrensburg, May 2011)

Overlooking the Schroon River in Warrensburg, the Grist Mill is a quaint and historic seasonal venue, located in a mill dating from 1820s. Intriguing from the outside, and with a good local buzz, this is the kind of restaurant that whenever you drive by it tends to be either crowded or closed.

The menu prices represent a slight splurge by local standards (plan on $50 a person even if you stay out of the wine list). Naturally, the apprehension about a place like the Grist Mill is, given the charming setting, that you're going to end up paying as much for the atmosphere as for the cuisine. Thus, our intrepid trio set off to determine if the food matched the location and insider hype.

Consider reservations mandatory in season and on weekends, and call ahead during the off-season to see if they are open. Regulars often specify that they wish to eat downstairs (we did), where five tables are perched above the river on a screened-in porch; the night air can get chilly, so bring a sweater or jacket from the car. The bar area has the most historic ambience, with an old fireplace and 19th century stonework on display. On our May visit, the river rushed by in a torrent more suited for whitewater rafting than for a romantic twilight backdrop; however, by summertime, this view represents a strong candidate for things like that all important third date. The first floor dining room possesses a more refined atmosphere, and the window tables offer a less elemental experience of the river as well—one that is climate controlled and free from any odd snippets of conversations shouted above the din. Clearly these make the best tables for those wanting to ensure a quiet meal.

Time for a Food Snob aphorism: Appetizers should be the gateway to a great meal, not the high point. Many restaurants put out good apps, but the main courses seem to suffer from neglect, wherein portion size is a substitute for craft. We started our meal by selecting pan-fried crab cakes, with grilled Belgian endive, and a cilantro and lime sauce; the cakes succeeded in not being overly breaded, stayed crisp on the outside, and the sauce complimented the crabmeat without adding either too much richness or spice. We also tried the beets and pan-seared scallops simply because Food Snob felt the dish couldn't possibly succeed without some unifying vinaigrette. While the scallops were indeed excellent, we wanted more than three of them, and the beets, as predicted, neither complemented nor detracted from the scallops. Overall, the appetizers were good, not quite great, and Food Snob's brow tightened in concern as he awaited the entrée, which, as far as he was concerned, would determine the verdict on the entire experience thumbs up or thumbs down. It's this kind of drama that makes the life of a food reviewer so exciting, and not, as most people think, the elaborate disguises worn to protect the critic from being identified.

Little did Chef Chris Lambeth know how much depended upon his Friday night main courses. For him, it was just another night, twelve years into his highly regarded operation; for us, a defining moment. In our self-important minds, he was facing his single most critical evaluation since graduating from culinary school at

Johnson & Wales. So let's start with *tournedos au poivre*, served with two sauces, one a magnificent veal demi-glace, rich with subtle tomato undertones; the second, a roasted red pepper coolie, had a lighter fresh touch. The beef itself came out just under medium-rare, and the quality of the cut was evident in both the flavor and perfect tenderness. We also tried the unique Grist Mill shrimp scampi, prepared with goat cheese, house-made oven roasted tomatoes (like sun-dried, but not), finished with Harvey's Bristol Cream, all served over fettuccini. Points were scored for the pasta being *al dente* and flavorful, more points were racked up for the inventiveness, wherein the tang of the goat cheese and the potency of the tomato accented the dish beautifully. The sherry, perhaps the most risky facet of the recipe, scored again and worked well with the other ingredients, and our concerns that it might be too sweet proved unwarranted.

Now, customarily, one of the dishes clearly outshines the others. On this particular occasion, as we turned our attention to the pan-seared halibut, served over a "spicy" shrimp Thai rice, we were pretty certain that another of Food Snob's aphorisms would apply: "Generally avoid Asian inspired dishes served at non-Asian restaurants, especially if they like to use the word eclectic." Okay, sure, the King of Siam might not recognize the authenticity of this rice, but damn it was good, okay, even fabulous. And the cilantro crème *fraiche* worked well to tie the dish together thematically. However, even more points accrue to the chef for selecting good suppliers and great ingredients, and, in the case of the halibut, by executing the basics of pan searing with aplomb, the flavor of the fish itself never being lost or drowned, but rather elevated, by the accompaniments.

In short, each dish was excellent, portions appropriate, and none of us could pick a clear winner as to best thing of the night. To pass another tip along, insiders rave about the herb-encrusted rack of lamb, stuffed with roasted garlic, spinach, Dijon mustard and bread crumbs, and then finished with rosemary *au jus*. This item, unavailable recently, is returning to the menu in the summer of 2011 thanks to popular request.

Dessert remained, not as a meal saver, but as a last potential stumbling block to culinary glory. We went with the homemade chocolate mousse Napoleon; one with raspberry sauce, and the other with a Bananas Foster sauce. We were immediately conquered. The mousse, strong milk chocolate sandwiched between a delectable wafer, produced a rare consensus as best dessert of the campaign. Indeed, even Napoleon's famous chef, Antonin Carême, father of *haute cuisine* and King of Chefs, would have nodded his head in approval at this confectionary masterpiece.

3. Café Adirondack (Pottersville, May 2011)

It took us far too long to hear the buzz about this quirky place, now in its fifth year. And there's a reason for it. People love it so much that, something like jealous suitors, they wish to keep its pleasures known only to themselves. It's an understandable instinct on one hand, stemming from a kind of Adirondack "prime directive" to protect the local culture from too much outside contact, whereby things might get spoiled. We admit that we too felt a temptation to exclude this information. Oh, what irony, if in praising a restaurant too highly, we ended up burying it. So dear reader, we pass the burden to you. Do not visit this place too often, do not share it with mere acquaintances, but only with true friends. Otherwise, mum's the word.

From the outside, the restaurant looks a bit rundown, like a Mom and Pop greasy spoon. We like the disguise, its modesty preventing most "drive by" customers from noticing. Only those with that sixth sense for good restaurants will turn on their blinkers and pull in here, although the number of cars could be a tip off. Note that the café is always closed Monday and Tuesdays (and Wednesdays in the off-season), and reservations are a wise precaution.

Once inside, the place does have a real café feel; and unlike a number of holes in the walls where sullen indifference is the order of the day, customers here are made to feel welcome immediately. The positive attitude is infectious. It's easy to see that people are having a good time; it's relaxed, unpretentious, fun. A collection of conversation pieces are tastefully displayed about on the walls, shelves, and cabinets, like old radios, pewter dishes, antique cameras, one man's junk we suppose. It looks as if they started with a curiosity shop before plunking in a restaurant. Table 12, our favorite, sits in a sort of private alcove that has an enormous bookshelf with an excellent selection of literature; it's clearly the place for former English majors or cocktail party dilettantes to impress a date.

Unless you bring your own alcohol—and we didn't see any corkage fee, but plenty of regulars brought their own wine—go with the refreshing homemade lemonade at a mere two dollars a glass. We started with two wonderful soups, the she-crab bisque and the spicy carrot-ginger, and both soups got better with each taste. The salad had homemade croutons and a nice selection of produce, and we tried all the homemade dressings, with the Ranch dressing a clear winner (and Food Snob usually hates it, irritatingly pronouncing it as "raunch" dressing).

The entrees were well-prepared and nicely presented. The filet with *béarnaise* sauce met expectations, the meat tender and the sauce at a proper consistency. The crab cakes came out crisp and meaty. The accompanying vegetables retained texture and flavor, clearly not frozen, and the rice was also well-executed. Perhaps a surprising star of the show was the "Chloe" potatoes—evidence of what the menu calls a Coastal Carolina influence—a combination of bacon, cheese and the famous ranch dressing that sounded like it would be overwhelmingly, but was instead truly delicious. (We even took an order home and had them for breakfast the next day, with eggs, and it proved to be an excellent idea).

Desserts are also homemade. The Grasshopper pie came with mint chocolate chip ice cream topped with chopped up peppermint patties, drizzled over with chocolate fudge, powdered sugar and whipped cream. It did not disappoint. The strawberry-rhubarb pie proved good as well, the crust crisp, and made a fine selection for those preferring tart to sweet at the end of the meal.

Now, we have to say that, in the course of this book, our server, Jessica, wins the prize for best in category, hands down. Her knowledge of the menu was excellent, and her descriptions of each dish helped us make informed choices. Friendly, efficient, and willing to engage in all sorts of ridiculous banter with Food Snob, she not only won him over, but seemed to make a difference at each table she covered. From now on, we are going to request her by name.

Overall, everything at Café Adirondack is very good, although those who want highly inventive or unusual cuisine won't really find that sort of thing here. Portions are ample and prices very reasonable, and without the bar tab, it keeps the night from getting expensive. We've had a few meals that served better pieces of culinary art, sure, but we'd be hard pressed to name a place where we enjoyed the entire experience more.

4. Friend's Lake Inn Restaurant (Chestertown, June 2011)

Historic Friend's Lake Inn has been a longstanding flagship of Adirondack dining; few of these landmarks remain. Dating back to the 1860's and running through the era of the grand Adirondack hotels, the Friend's Lake Inn features a dining room that retains an elegant late nineteenth-century feel with a painted tin ceiling and soft lighting enhancing the evocative Victorian feel.

Currently, the Inn exhibits the most impressive wine list in the region, boasting over 25,000 bottles and 2,200 types of wine, from Napa and Sonoma to Burgundy and Bordeaux. The owners stress their Wine Spectator Award; very few restaurants nationally meet the criteria to earn one. We have to admit that there is a great vicarious interest in seeing what sort of folks plunk down $1200 for a *Grands Crus,* and, after all, we just want one tiny sip…but the clientele, an interesting mix of splurging locals and well-heeled out of towners, certainly can be entertaining for those who can't resist a little people watching.

Chef Matthew Bolton and Sous Chef Scott Dewar feature what they call New American cuisine. For a good example of this, start with what everyone says is the best appetizer on the menu, the Scallop and Lobster Stuffed Corn Crêpe. The pan-seared scallops are served in a delicious vanilla *beurre blanc,* pecan and pistachio praline with chopped scallions. Yes, it's a sweet and delicate creation—and here the lobster works wonders— but it's not excessively sugary. Certainly the dish ranked as one of the best appetizers of the tour. We also had a chanterelle and drunken goat lasagna, which sounded interesting but didn't rank as highly; the goat cheese didn't impart the tartness I suppose we were expecting from the porcini cream sauce. If you're doing wines, try the cheese plate, a French tradition, which offers several selections from which you can choose a few; here the sommelier might assist in making some interesting pairings.

The entrees were very ample by fine dining standards. We had a pork tenderloin served in a Dijon mustard sauce, and a seafood mélange in a saffron sauce, with corn and peas, all served over with a spaghetti squash (as if the squash were the pasta, very cool idea). The pork tenderloin, while good, would have been better if the mustard hadn't been as sweet, which took the edge off the dish for Food Snob. The fried potatoes that came on the side with the pork merited special attention; crisp, caramelized, superb, these stole the show. We all agreed that the best thing about the seafood dish was the novelty of the spaghetti squash; the mildness of the saffron sauce seemed to be playing it safe. For dessert, we had the tableside Bananas Foster, always a good show.

As an overall destination, the Inn would seem to be a perfect romantic getaway for urbanites, who would find the prices to be very reasonable, especially the weekend room and meal package. If wines are your thing, then this is *de rigueur*. For the budget conscious, the Friend's Lake Inn also has a wine bar which serves New American cuisine at more reasonable prices, and the menu does have some overlap. (Note: The Friends Lake Inn caters to adult tastes and is not a child friendly environment). The Inn is also very popular with cross-country skiers.

5. Brunetto's (Warrensburg, June 2011)

If you're going to go to Brunetto's, bring a big appetite. A few hundred yards from the Northway Exit 23, with a sign that is hard to spot, you can drive past this place on Route 9 numerous times without noticing it. Locals endorse it enthusiastically, and for those vacationing in Lake George a few miles away, Brunetto's makes an easy ten or fifteen minute drive. Now, for some reason, Brunetto's no longer takes reservations, so during summer evenings a wait is quite possible. The bar portion of the restaurant is actually more atmospheric, so have a round while you wait.

The dining room, done in a merlot color and possessing a large fireplace at one end, holds about 12 tables, but is otherwise dark and uninteresting. Being late in our restaurant tour, we've become more and more jaded about "standard Adirondack restaurant fare" and Brunetto's covered most of the greatest hits like crab cakes, prime rib, sirloin steaks, chicken *parmigiana*, etc. Brunetto's did offer some items not seen everywhere else, like a liver pate appetizer. However, we've been getting the crab cakes as a means of comparing places, and Brunetto's clearly offered the largest crab cake any of us had ever seen. Somehow they managed to get it crisp, despite being about five inches in diameter, and the sauce wasn't bad either. Six oysters on the half-shell represented another less usual offering; they slid down easily enough with the cocktail sauce and lemon, pleasantly cold, but the oysters themselves seemed ordinary. Interestingly, Brunetto's charges for bread, which we ordered, and can say that, all in all, tasty but maybe not worth the extra charge or stomach space. Our neighbor's fried clams looked like a meal sized portion, and appeared crisp, and we wished we'd ordered those instead of the oysters. The steamed mussels also looked appealing.

In general, Brunetto's eschews inventiveness and creativity in favor of consistent execution and large portion size. The menu plays it safe, to the "more is good" local expectation. Most of the seafood dishes come one of three ways, either broiled (some in white wine and butter), fried, or blackened. At our server's recommendation, we tried the Fresh Canadian Salmon, blackened. It arrived crisp and spicy, cooked through but not to the point of dryness, and the amount seemed like a double portion of what you'd expect in the city. The chicken *piccata* with linguine scored highly with our local survey group. Food Snob felt it rated as good but nothing transcendent—he wanted more punch from the lemon and capers. Again, the amount of food dictated that we took half of it home with us.

The desserts come from J&S Watkins, a fairly well-known Malta bakery. Most people generally don't have any room left, so don't make dessert a priority here, as our raspberry chocolate rumble was adequate for the sweet tooth, but nothing memorable. Brunetto's represents a step up from the Lake George strip, and you won't feel ripped off. Enormous portions, fair prices, and good food. Locals praise it for the dependability "when it's open."

6. Hague Firehouse Restaurant (Hague, May 2011)

Picturesque, with the Hague Brook running past and flowing into Lake George, the town of Hague seems like an idyllic little place to spend the summer, replete with a great beach on the lake. Located in the former firehouse, the restaurant has brick walls adorned with local artists work, and an attractive u-shaped bar. The only knock is that the high ceiling bounces rather than absorbs the noise, so it can sound a bit lively if the bar gets crowded. The back deck has a great view of the brook, so sit there for conversation on pleasant evenings.

The menu won't win any prizes for novelty, in part because to stay in business it has to draw a local repeat crowd while balancing against the preferences of some out-of-towners. However, the food is well-prepared, portions are large, and prices are fairly reasonable. We tried the Yellowfin tuna with island spices (fresh ginger, wasabi, soy glaze) and arugula to start, and found it pleasing. An unexpected hit, given its endless appearances on local menus, was the chicken *parmigiana*; here you get a vast portion of tender chicken, perfectly breaded and crisply fried, with pasta that was not overcooked. The New York strip, a cut of meat that Food Snob finds only slightly less pedestrian than sirloin, was also tender and flavorful. The Jerk chicken, a frequent special, proved less satisfying than the usual suspects.

The Hague Firehouse is one of the few dining choices within miles; fortunately, it is a good one. Nothing over the top, but definitely solid, and the kind of place that such a lovely spot needs to have around.

7. George's Place for Steak (Lake George, May 2011)

Opposite Lake George Village on the eastern shore, George's is a top notch Adirondack Retro destination—you might even call it pretty swanky—with a beautiful dark log cabin interior, mounted heads of game animals high along the walls, and a cutting edge menu circa 1955. Locals flock to the place, and if you sit on the second stage of the restaurant, you can pick up tons of gossip as patrons throw back a few cocktails. The service is unfashionably friendly, and they *might* just actually care how you are doing. Seniors and families tend to come early, well before 6:30, when meals are discounted significantly from the prime time prices. George's takes reservations, so please call ahead during July and August.

Yes, we started our meal with a visit to the salad bar. Now, we've got to say, that having a well-stocked salad bar is so retro chic that we were excited. The nostalgic pleasures of sticking a large spoon into a pile of garbanzo beans or lentils, sprinkling as many damned bacon bits as you want, "tonging" through the chilled lettuce for the most appealing pieces, throwing on entirely too much dressing, well, it made us feel like kids again on some epic summer trip. Not that any of the components rated highly, but who really cares? Food Snob lamented that a stellar homemade dressing would have kicked this up a notch, but ultimately we would learn that it's probably best not to go overboard—vast portions lurked ahead— and the salad was only the tip of the iceberg.

We've been on a French onion soup kick all tour, in part because it's a part of nearly every menu in the Adirondacks, and gives us another staple to judge everyone. The pandemonium that would break out in the Park if this item were removed from the menus is hard to estimate. However, a place claiming to make great steak better be able to bring a good crock of it, and in this, George's did not disappoint. Darkly caramelized onions, strong but not overly salty broth, and layers (not a single piece) of cheese, browned and crisped, made this a strong candidate for best in show.

As for entrees, let's make this as simple as possible. If you go to George's, at least half of your party must be there for the prime rib. The king cut came out looking as large as the Brontosaurus meat that would tip over Fred Flintstone's car. An enormously thick cut seemingly 50% larger than the 24 ounces advertised, it came perfectly cooked through, pink, and wonderfully tender. Certainly, this prime rib would garner our blue ribbon if we handed out that sort of thing—so, there, consider George's as the winner of the Best Traditional Prime Rib, 2011. Food Snob said that it compared favorably with some of the most expensive steakhouses in the country, you know, the famous ones that advertise in airline magazines. Ask for the horseradish sauce, and get the baked potato. Some traditions persist for a reason.

We also tried the jumbo shrimp stuffed with Alaskan crab meat, which were very good if basic, and locals love the surf and turf. George's can be rather expensive, so if you can go early, do so and take advantage of the special. The dessert menu also features homemade cream pies, not something you see every day, and we particularly enjoyed the tell-tale crisp crust on our slice of Boston Cream pie.

Lastly, one can't help but notice that the owner is very involved in running her cat rescue operation, even going so far as to offer customers who donate $50 to the shelter an equivalent coupon redeemable at the restaurant. So, animal lovers who are uncomfortable with the antique taxidermy can expiate any sense of guilt with a quick donation to save some contemporary cats.

8. Caffé Vero (Lake George, April 2011)

Located in the heart of the Lake George Village strip, this is a place that Food Snob routinely ventures off the Northway to stop and visit. Why? Well, he feels strongly that it is the best coffee in the Adirondacks. The lattés and cappuccinos are wonderful—not bitter or acidic, but robust enough—and are beautifully served with a lavish swirl pattern in the foam. The house coffee is medium roasted, mellow, smooth, easy on the stomach, yet strongly flavorful.

You can also get a pretty good breakfast here. Try one of the breakfast burritos if you're hungry, but the thing locals most rave about is the pancakes. The café is bigger than it looks from the front, and has a fireplace and several tables in the back. The owners are earnest, hard-working and friendly, and the service has been, so far, consistently good. We haven't tried lunch, but there is some buzz about the soup being a must.

9. Barnsider Smokehouse Restaurant (Lake George, June 2010)

Along with Sushi Yoshi (up Route 9 towards Glens Falls), the Barnsider ranks as one of the best casual family dining places in Lake George. Formerly a family run deli and liquor store, it went barbecue in 1991. Run by a father and son team, the Pagnottas take pride in their barbecue recipes, which features some Memphis style dry rubbing and other arcane smoking processes. Serving on both the first and second floor, as well as on the deck in the summer, the Barnsider gets noisy and busy, just as a BBQ place should. A small bar in the front of the house pours Saranac beers on tap, as well as their own "Barnsider Smokehouse Ale."

The Barnsider features smoky ribs that fall off the bone, crisp on the outside, moist and tender on the inside. We couldn't resist trying the crispy green bean fries for an appetizer (better than you might think actually) and the barbecue potato skins. We also tried the pulled pork and baby back ribs. While Food Snob felt the meat was "overly smoky" because it was "the end of the night," the rest of us had no complaints. The service was excellent, and they were happy to accommodate our last minute arrival.

We recommend the three course special, with choice of appetizer, entrée, and dessert for $19.99. If you like the sauce, bottles are available to go.

10. The Place (Chestertown, September 2011)

Ahh, nostalgia. Almost nothing has changed in the 30 years or so that Food Snob has been coming to The Place, from the wall decorations to the selections at the bar. Okay, the salad dressing isn't as good as it once was, a delicacy that the young budding Snob would drink with a spoon and invariably spill dressing on the plastic redchecked table clothes, provoking some consternation from his grandmother. But the wonderful sauce is exactly the same recipe at this family run joint, and it should remain a carefully guarded secret.

Sure, you can start with some garlic bread and perhaps a garden salad (mostly iceberg), but don't fill up. You're really here for only one thing, the *parmigiana,* gloriously done in that upstate New York American-Italian style. Get the sampler plate, and try the eggplant parm, and either the veal or chicken. Portions are such that you might take a fair amount of food home, and the prices are a downright bargain. We often call ahead on our way up north and get our orders to go.

11. Frederick's (Bolton Landing, February, 2011)

Frederick's is the place locals will usually tell you to go, particularly if hanging out is as important as the dining out. People are welcoming and talkative, and you can get a sense of local personalities and the community as you have a draft or two. Owned by a brother and sister team, both graduates of Johnson and Wales in Rhode Island, Stuart and Connie Maxam Smith have been running this operation for over twenty years. In the off-season, it stays open every day, something appreciated by residents and a mean feat economically.

The main room with the large wooden bar and cozy fireplace is very inviting, and we decided to hang out at the bar. The environment proved conducive to conversation—we got a pretty interesting local history lesson on Bolton Landing and Lake George—and we chatted with Stuart as well, turns out he briefly dated someone we know, and all in all, it's that kind of place.

The food is just about average, and sometimes rises above. Our bar neighbors recommended an appetizer called "Hoopes," a variety of fried chicken wings crisped up by being placed under the broiler at the end. These were quite good—hadn't had them before—and those who don't like sauce-drenched messy wings might really enjoy these. We liked the rosemary bread, but thought the French onion soup was not sufficiently broiled off. For dinner, the chicken pot pie represented reasonable comfort food, and set the record for the dish that took the longest to cool off. The shrimp scampi rated well, largely because the addition of sun-dried tomatoes really enhanced the dish. The steak sandwich, however, had too many chewy bits to endorse.

Frederick's flourishes in the summer as the outdoor deck is quite popular and lively. The raw bar has many local advocates, and sounds like it might be worth a try. Live music is available on many evenings, and festivities can go quite late into the night.

12. The Loft (Lake George)

Situated at the intersection of Route 9 and 149 on the edge of the Adirondack Park, this is a burger shack. Once inside, it turns into the North Country's version of "cheeburger, cheeburger" the famous *Saturday Night Live* skit featuring Dan Akroyd and John Belushi.

Adding to the comedy, the first time we wandered in here, they had run out of hamburgers. If that happens, leave, though some people seem to like the cheesesteaks.

Folks, this is a top ten hamburger. It's cheap. Bring the kids, sit at the picnic tables or on the hood of the car, and enjoy. The fries are great too. It's an authentic joint and sure beats the corporate burgers elsewhere.

13. Anywhere's A Better Place than Here (Chestertown, Oct. 2010)

Woody Allen once exclaimed that 90% of life is just showing up. The Adirondack restaurant corollary is that 90% of the job is just managing to stay open. It just so happened on a Monday in the off-season that we couldn't find a place to eat and nearly drove past the place (only four parking spaces). So we pulled in, puzzled a bit by the name, but determined to give it our business anyway. The bar is large and intriguing, so we sat there and enjoyed some drafts.

"Anywhere" has the earmarks of a local joint with character. You can't go wrong with the burgers, probably among the top ten in the Park. We had a salad with vinaigrette that was shockingly good; honestly, the best salad dressing of the year, shaming much more expensive restaurants. "Why is it that good salad dressing is so hard to find?" Food Snob lamented after decrying "pre-packaged laziness" for a few minutes. We've also tried the barbecue, which is relatively ordinary, but can satisfy a craving, and the crab cakes weren't bad.

The prices are inexpensive, locals recommend the fish on Fridays, and the burgers are on special on Monday nights.

The Algonquin, Bolton Landing (out-take, May, 2011)

An Open Letter to Rachael R.:

This is your fan Food Snob. I am terribly sorry to have to report the demise of a restaurant because it seems such a spectacular shame.

Not only you, but others, have raved about The Algonquin in years' past as being one of their favorite places on Lake George. Indeed, it still possesses the million dollar view of Huddle Bay. The boats come in and out, and sometimes, as a wooden Chris Craft approaches the docks in the fading twilight, a Gatsby-like sense of wonder commences, and evokes the ghostliness of lost summers, those by-gone parties and that carefree laughter that once echoed over the evening's still waters. And I am still haunted by visions of you, sitting at my very table, raving about the sublime "Fish Point" sandwich which I too, at last, would experience. I wanted that bond with you, our local Adirondacker made good, and me, by contrast, toiling in anonymity.

My feeling of serenity at least survived the first course, the New England Clam chowder, buttery but not starchy, and flavorful, all in all a very fine commencement to the meal. Then the trouble began. An otherwise flavorful crab cake, browned with grill marks, proved soggy, which seemed inexplicable, given the speed of the service— how could it have lost its perfection under the lamps in such short order? A shame, because the mildly zesty remoulade also tasted good, the citrus cutting the richness back in splendid fashion. Okay, these things happen, it's not ominous, recovery is possible.

I held out hope Rachael, I really did. I believed that one of the greatest fish sandwiches of my lifetime was coming. I had a fleeting image of you waterskiing in the lake from the same television episode, my last happy thoughts for the evening. When the "sandwich" arrived, there were not tears of joy, no rapture, but rather an overwhelming despair. What was promised as an "open-faced" delicacy appeared as a bald-faced lie. Oh, I assure you, this would have ranked as one of the worst seafood dishes I'd ever eaten. But the extent of the crash, like the end of the roaring twenties themselves, from such top-lofty expectations to such spiritually crushing reality, magnified the cruelty unbearably. Oh, from the sublime to the ridiculous is but a piece of Dover Sole so badly breaded with egg that it tasted like mushy, fishy, scrambled eggs on soggy toast. I felt badly, of course, for my server, for my companions, for myself, and even for the fishermen who wait in boats off the Cliffs of Dover to catch these soles. But, most of all, I felt badly for you, because I understand. Yes, it's going to happen to me too. We endorse a place in this region we love, put our time and reputations at stake, our fans trust us, and then they end up with a dining experience like this. I know that someone in 2014, using the 2011 edition of this guide, will write us with such vitriol that we will feel terrible, and in response we will mutter protests of innocence that we did our best at the time.

There are a couple of things you *can* do for me to make this better. One, have your people call the Algonquin people. Tell them you expected more, you expected them to uphold your endorsement, and you wanted a real effort never to let you down. Tell them to take down your quote from the website, and take down Andy Rooney's too. Tell them just because they have a great view doesn't mean they can get away with this. And, two, let's have dinner sometime. I'll wear my rather smashing white linen suit that some people feel looks ridiculous, but I think otherwise. Together we can find that great good restaurant on the Lake George waterfront, where the million dollar view and the million dollar flavor collide in an orgiastic moment that only cuisine lovers like you and I can fully know. Afterward, we will board that antique wooden boat (have your people rent it) and we will motor outward into the Adirondack evening, each of us taking turns regaling the other with tales of dining sure to bore anyone but us. Until then, best wishes, I know it's not your fault.

P.S. And, stay out of the Boathouse Restaurant just down the road from here as well. It was even worse.

SOUTH/EAST ADIRONDACK LOCAL LOWDOWN

Bolton Landing

Cate's Italian Garden

4952 Main Street
Bolton Landing, NY 12814
(518) 644-2041
www.catesitaliangarden.com

Local Lowdown: "Quaint, cute place" .... You can sit outside or inside.... "Good wine selection" .... "Great atmosphere, friendly staff" .... "Pizza is good."

Fredericks Restaurant

4970 Lake Shore Drive
Bolton Landing, NY 12814
(518) 644-3484
www.fredericksrestaurant.com

Local Lowdown: Live music during the summer.... "Good soups" out by one of the fireplaces in the winter.... "Love their crispy wings and homemade bread."

Hometown Diner

5116 Lake Shore Drive
Bolton Landing, NY 12814
(518) 644-9038

Local Lowdown: "Definitely a local hang-out" .... "Good for breakfast/lunch" .... "I Love the Hometown Diner" .... "It's the Sunday morning thing to do."

Mr. Brown's Pub (Located in the Sagamore)

110 Sagamore Road
Bolton Landing, NY 12814
(866) 385-6221
www.thesagmore.com

Local Lowdown: An inexpensive way to check out the posh Sagamore Resort.... Good pub food, some interesting beers.... "Too many *au pairs* and kids" .... Rachel Ray reputedly was a manager here.

Pumpernickel's Restaurant

4571 Lake Shore Drive
Bolton Landing, NY 12814
(518) 644-2106
www.pumpernickels.com

Local Lowdown: The only authentic German restaurant in the area; many people feel this is the best place to eat in Bolton Landing.... Owns and displays the largest cuckoo clock in the United States! .... Open for dinner late June through Labor Day.... On our 2012 list.... "Good Oktoberfest!"

Ryefield Bar & Restaurant
4949 Lake Shore Drive
Bolton Landing, NY 12814
(518) 644-9107

Local Lowdown: "Good wait staff" .... "Some feel food is pricey for what you get" .... Building currently for sale.

Wooden Barrel
4571 Lake Shore Drive
Bolton Landing, NY 12814
(518) 644-2106

Local Lowdown: Owned by the same owners of Pumpernickel's.... Open year-round.... Late night bar with pool table and darts.... "Good beers!"

Chestertown

Anywhere's a Better Place to Be

6332 State Route 9
Chestertown, NY 12817
(518) 494-5888

Local Lowdown: "Good burgers and salads" .... "Go for cocktails!"

Friends Lake Inn

963 Friends Lake Road
Chestertown, NY 12817
(518) 494-4751
www.friendslake.com

Local Lowdown: Beautiful setting.... "Very nice" .... "Their wine list is like a phone book—it's that extensive!" .... "Expensive" .... "It's a great romantic get-away!"

Main Street Ice Cream Parlor

6339 Main Street
Chestertown, NY 12817
(518) 494-7940
www.loonyaboutadirondacks.com/Ice-Cream-Parlor.html

Local Lowdown: 1950's nostalgic atmosphere.... "Good burgers & Ruebens" .... Big menu for an ice cream place.... Kid-friendly.

O.P Frederick's Restaurant

5064 Route 8
Chestertown, NY 12817
(518) 494-4141
www.viop.net

Local Lowdown: "Good, real Adirondack atmosphere" .... "Staff is friendly" .... A large variety on the menu.... "Quaint" .... "A good family restaurant."

The Place

5156 Route 8
Chestertown, NY 12817-3612
(518) 494-3390
www.theplaceitalianrestaurant.com

Local Lowdown: "Great place for anything *parmagiana*!" ....
"Family place" .... "Huge portions!" .... Closed Tuesdays and
Wednesdays.... Owner's a big fisherman.

Crown Point

Gunnison Lakeshore Orchards

3208 NYS Route 9N
Crown Point, NY 12928
(518) 597-3134

Local Lowdown: Food Snob says these were, in 2008, the best pies
in the region.... Slated for follow-up 2012 review.... Apple cider
doughnuts and fruit turnovers also superb.

Frenchman's Family Dining

2749 Main Street
Crown Point, NY 12928
(518) 597-3545

Local Lowdown: Ice cream stand/diner food.... "Good friendly
service" .... "Homey."

Hague

Hague Firehouse Restaurant

9813 Graphite Mountain Road
Hague, NY 12836
(518) 543-6266
www.haguefirehouse.com/index.html

Local Lowdown: "Fun local place" .... "Good food" .... Sit outside overlooking the Hague Brook.... "Nice big bar" .... "Good-sized portions" .... Creative "gourmet" specials.

Lake George

Barnsider Smokehouse Restaurant

10 Mountain View Lane
Lake George, NY 12845
(518) 668-5268
www.barnsider.com

Local Lowdown: "Friendly staff" .... "Good BBQ" .... Small bar, can sit inside or out on the deck.... "Great ribs—full of flavor and very crispy!" .... "The 3-course dinner special is a good deal."

Bistro Le Roux

668 Route 149
Lake George, NY 12845
(518) 798-2982
www.bistroleroux.com

Local Lowdown: Right off route 149 (by the outlets).... Newer restaurant.... "Great atmosphere and friendly service" .... Can get big or small portions for dinner entrees.

Blue Moose Tavern & Restaurant
Corner of Route 9 & Glen Lake Road
Queensbury, NY
(518) 761-2583

Local Lowdown: "Good Prime Rib" .... Live music on Fridays and Saturdays.... Fun karaoke on Wednesdays.... "Good bar atmosphere."

Caffé Vero

185 Canada Street
Lake George, NY 12845-1401
(518) 668-5800
http://caffeverocoffee.com

Local Lowdown: "Best cup of coffee in the north!"

Docksider Restaurant
298 Glen Lake Road
Lake George, NY 12845
(518) 792-3534
www.glenlakedocksider.com

Local Lowdown: "Good atmosphere" .... "Nice size dinners" .... "Sitting outside is a must!" .... You can boat or drive to the restaurant.... Good deals on weekday specials!

Duffy's Restaurant

20 Amherst Street
Lake George, NY 12845
(518)668-5323

Local Lowdown: "A nice place to sit on the patio, listen to live entertainment, and have a view of Lake George" .... "Awesome chicken wings and great bar!" .... Music on the deck during summer season.... "Great hang-out" .... "Everyone knows Duffy's."

East Cove

Route 9L and Beach Road
Lake George, NY 12845
(518) 668-5265
www.eastcove.com

Local Lowdown: Formerly a "Local Favorite" .... Serves coleslaw and bread.... "Get the Surf & Turf!" .... Retro—big Scotch list (seventeen single malt scotches).... "Good to go to if George's Place for steak is too busy" .... Dropped off in the last two years, so be warned.... Open year round.... Sunday brunch.

Farmhouse at the Top of the World

441 Lockhart Mountain Road
Lake George, NY 12845
(518) 668-2062
www.topoftheworldgolfresort.com/dining.asp

Local Lowdown: Beautiful view.... Husband and wife owners; wife is the farmer, husband is the chef.... "They do a lot of weddings" .... Beer pairing and wine pairing dinner options.... "Be adventurous and try the chef tasting."

George's Place for Steak

3857 Route 9L
Lake George, NY 12845
(518) 668-5482

Local Lowdown: "Great salad bar!" .... "Unbelievable steaks!"
"Early bird specials" .... "King-size prime rib is bigger than
your head!"

The Loft

3 New York 149
Lake George, NY 12845-3500
(518) 793-2296

Local Lowdown: Burger joint near the outlets.... Looks like a
little barn on the corner of Route 9 and Route 149.... "Good place
to stop for a quick bite to eat" .... No frills here—no website or
take-out menu available.... "Great food, low prices."

Log Jam Restaurant

1484 State Route 9
Lake George, NY 12845
(518) 798-1155
www.logjamrestaurant.com

Local Lowdown: In the midst of all the outlet shopping.... "Great
salad bar and wines" .... "Best lobster tails in the Adirondacks"
.... "Service is out of this world!" .... Serving lunch and dinner....
"Great atmosphere."

Mama Riso's Restaurant

PO Box 132
Lake George, NY 12845
(518) 668-2550
www.menumart.com/mamarisos

Local Lowdown: "Awesome veal dishes!" .... "Best Italian food in Lake George!" .... Open since the 1980's.... "Good atmosphere, family friendly."

Mario's Restaurant

429 Canada Street
Lake George NY 12845
(518) 668-2665
www.marioslakegeorge.com

Local Lowdown: Has been owned by one family since 1957! .... "Good Italian fare!" .... "Staff is great!" .... "Good bread" .... Reservations suggested (can be done online).

The Silo

537 Aviation Road
Queensbury, NY 12804
(518) 798-1900
www.thesiloqueensbury.com

Local Lowdown: Locally famous, just off Northway exit 18.... Brunch recommended by everyone! .... "A local landmark" .... "Good hot turkey sandwich" .... "Take your mother or grandmother here for breakfast."

Tamarack Inn
440 Canada Street
Lake George, NY 12845
(518) 668-5400

Local Lowdown: "Good for breakfast" .... "Food can be inconsistent" .... "Nice people and good atmosphere."

Lake Luzerne

Longhorn Café
1379 Lake Avenue
Lake Luzerne, NY 12846
(518) 696-5655

Local Lowdown: "Good stuff" .... Known for their burgers and steaks.... Kids welcome.

The Painted Pony
703 Howe Road
Lake Luzerne, NY 12846
(518) 696-2421
www.paintedponyrodeo.com/texas-bbq.asp

Local Lowdown: Texas-style buffet BBQ.... Five miles outside of Lake George.... "Professional rodeo" .... "Cheesy, but fun!" .... Country Western dancing too!

The Waterhouse
85 Lake Avenue
NY 12846-2326
(518) 696-3115

Local Lowdown: Known for their prime rib and seafood dishes.... "It's nice to sit outside."

Minerva/Olmstedville

Little Nony's Bakery
1385 Route 29
Olmstedville, NY 12857
(518)251-2289

Local Lowdown: Homemade doughnuts, cakes, chicken salad.... "Awesome cinnamon buns!" .... They have sandwiches too.... Serve breakfast and lunch.

Lucky Leprechaun
612 Morse Memorial Highway
Olmstedville, NY 12857
(518) 251-3380

Local Lowdown: Italian place—not Irish.... "Good homemade pizza" .... "Great place for bar-type food" .... Ambiance is filled with leprechauns and is very green....

Owl at Twilight
1322 Route 29
Olmstedville, NY 12857
(518) 251-4696

Local Lowdown: Reopened in 2010.... Less expensive than before.... Great for a romantic, good meal! .... Food can be on the spicy side, very good, great quality, nice people.... "Wonderful!" .... Hours are erratic; must call ahead.

Sporty's Bar
1723 Route 28N
Minerva, NY 12851
(518)251-5260
www.sportysirondukesaloon.com

Local Lowdown: Family-run and big in the community.... "Best bar ever—you don't have to drive home, you can rent a cabin!" .... "They go through a lot of beer there" .... Events throughout the year—bike shows, auctions, charity fund-raisers, Turkey Trot, helicopter rides, etc.... Get a copy of their event calendar! .... Cabin rentals in summer.... "One of the finest biker bars."

Pottersville

Black Bear
7882 Route 9
Pottersville, NY 12860
(518)494-9972

Local Lowdown: A popular quick stop to eat right off of exit 26 of the Northway.... "Big place for bikers" to stop too.... Open for breakfast, lunch, and dinner.... It's been around for about sixty years!

Café Adirondack

8015 Route 9
Pottersville, NY 12860
(518) 494-5800
www.cafeadirondack.com

Local Lowdown: Less than a mile from exit 26 off the Northway.... "Outstanding in all departments" .... "Good food at a reasonable price!" .... B.Y.O.B.

Schroon Lake

Drake's Restaurant

1299 Route 9
Schroon Lake, NY 12870
(518) 532-9040
www.drakesmotel.com/restaurant

Local Lowdown: "Good seafood and steaks" .... Open Mother's Day Weekend through Columbus Day.... "Get the filet mignon!" .... Reservations recommended on weekends.

Flanagan's Pub & Grill

1067 US Route 9 (Main Street)
Schroon Lake, NY 12870
(518) 532-9096

Local Lowdown: "Penny who runs this place is fantastic" .... "Best grasshoppers!" .... Local gathering spot.... "Great time" .... "Pub food and service are good!" .... "Good for snowmobilers."

Morningstar
1079 Us Route 9
Schroon Lake, NY 12870
(518) 532-0707
www.morningstarbistro.net

Local Lowdown: Known for their crêpes, unique soups, and creative wraps.... "Terrific bistro fare" .... "Good yummy sandwiches and good soups with side salad" .... "Perfect for a bite to eat after hiking" .... Gift shop.... "Great atmosphere!"

Suzie Q's Adirondack Grill
148 Tannery Road
Brant Lake, NY 12815
(518) 494-4381
http://jimbosclub.com/suzieq

Local Lowdown: "Good burgers" .... Beautiful log cabin feeling with high ceilings.... Off exit 25 of the Northway.... Serving breakfast, lunch and dinner.... Closed Mondays.

Ticonderoga

Adam's Ribs
117 Burgoyne Road
Ticonderoga, NY 12883
(518) 585-6388

Local Lowdown: BBQ place.... "Delicious food" .... Pub food and full dinners available.... "Reasonably priced."

Burleigh House
120 Montcalm Street
Ticonderoga, NY 12883
(518) 585-9138
www.burleighhouse.net

Local Lowdown: "Great diner" .... "Colorful bar. "

Carillon Restaurant
872 State Route 9N
Ticonderoga, NY 12883
(518) 585-7657
www.carillonrestaurant.com

Local Lowdown: Known for their steak dinners and seafood dinners.... Serves dinner starting at 4 p.m.... "Good mushrooms on filet and escargot" .... Closed on Wednesdays.

Corner Café
110 Lake George Avenue
Ticonderoga, NY 12883
(518) 585-2896

Local Lowdown: "Best hidden diner ever!" .... "Good prices and really nice people run it."

Fort View Inn
325 State Route 22
Ticonderoga, NY 12883
(518) 585-7767
www.carillonrestaurant.com

Local Lowdown: Great view, right on the lake.... "Good food" .... A little pricey" .... "Good chicken wings."

Hot Biscuit Diner
14 Montcalm Street
Ticonderoga, NY 12883
(518) 585-3483
http://hotbiscuitdiner.com

Local Lowdown: Known for their "basket meals" .... "Super friendly staff" .... Known for their chicken and biscuits, corned-beef hash, and strawberry shortcake.... "Social gathering place."

Treadway's Pub
1162 Route 9N
Ticonderoga, NY 12883
(518) 585-2866

Local Lowdown: Sports bar.... Pool table.... "Good tap selection and bar food."

Wagon Wheel
1065 Wicker Street
Ticonderoga, NY 12883
(518) 585-7755

Local Lowdown: "Consistently fantastic" .... "A favorite of the locals" .... "Good breakfast" .... "Very reasonable prices."

Wind-chill Factory

1065 Wicker Street
Ticonderoga, NY 12883
(518) 585-3044
www.windchillfactory.com

Local Lowdown: Ice cream, pretzels, hot dogs, and Michigans....
"A family tradition!" .... "A greasy goodness fest."

Warrensburg

Brunetto's

3579 Route 9
Warrensburg, NY 12885
(518) 623-1041

Local Lowdown: They don't take reservations.... You'll "definitely
have to wait" on weekends.... Caesar salad: "mmm" .... Get the
chicken piccata.

George Henry's

3735 Route 9
Warrensburg, NY 12885
(518) 623-5186

Local Lowdown: All you can eat Chicken Wings $7.99 on
Tuesday nights! .... "Good hot turkey sandwich" .... "Very local
bar" .... Family-run.... "Good choices of beer" .... Parking lot fills
up fast, but you can park along the side road too.

Grist Mill on the Schroon

Top 46

100 River Street
Warrensburg, NY 12885
(518) 623-8005
www.menumart.com/gristmill

Local Lowdown: Fine dining.... "Sit down in the bar area for better view and cooler atmosphere" .... "Good portions" .... "If you're in the Lake George area, you should definitely make a trip to the Grist Mill" .... "Outstanding food and service!" .... Not open in winter—opens Mother's Day weekend.

Jacob & Toney's IGA

3872 Main Street
Warrensburg, NY 12885
(518) 668- 9543

Local Lowdown: "Meat Store of the North!" .... Ninety years in business—weekly meat specials.... "Best sandwiches, good value!" .... "They are huge!" .... "Awesome meat selection" .... Good prices and homemade bread.

Oscar's Smokehouse

22 Raymond Lane
Warrensburg, NY 12885-1160
(518) 623-3431
www.oscarssmokedmeats.com

Local Lowdown: Not a restaurant.... The beef jerky is "out of this world!" .... "Everyone stops for their meat on their way to their camps!" .... Been in business for over sixty years.... Supplier to many of the best restaurants in region.

Adirondack Eats

CENTRAL REGION:

Blue Mountain Lake

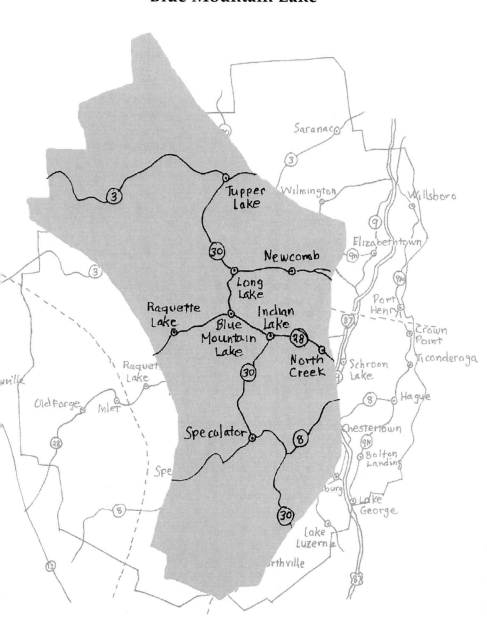

Featured Reviews:

1. barVino (North Creek, August 2010)

BarVino is barNone one of our favorite dining places in the mountains; an intimate artsy ambience, excellent food, great wines and interesting draft beers make this a must visit. One of the showpieces of the revitalized North Creek downtown, barVino is proof that the "foodie revolution" is taking hold in the Adirondacks. Fresh choice ingredients, most locally raised and some grown in their own summer garden, are a fundamental key to barVino's success. Chefs Luke Bowers and Kevin Gardner—both of whom received their training at La Posada in Sante Fe, New Mexico— have shaken off the culture shock and have embraced the offerings of local farms such as Nettle Meadow or Juniper Hill. Each chef exhibits a discerning palate and solid creative instincts, all the while avoiding pretentious over-reaches.

We also like the atmosphere and vibe; warm colors and high old tin ceilings that bounce back just the right amount of buzz. Paintings by local artists, a new set each month, are featured on the walls and add a little slice of Bohemia to the mix. The bar itself features a good selection of wines available by the glass, more than a two dozen or so available from an intriguing looking set of Napa-style wine taps. It's an absolutely great system for those who want to pair different wines to each plate, and our server offered excellent guidance. We liked the Museum Tampranillo, a Spanish wine, fruity with hints of dark cherry and slight tannin finish, to recommend but one. BarVino also has 12 draft beers on tap, and hops lovers should enjoy the regularly featured Dogfish Head 60 minute I.P.A, made by a craft brewer located in Delaware, (home state of owners Mike, Anna, and Luke Bowers) as well as Davidson Brothers, made locally in Glens Falls, which produces a first-rate brown ale. For those who like lighter or less hoppy choices, Bitburger Pilsener, a German beer rarely seen in these parts, made a welcome appearance on tap. So, yes, it is a great place to have a couple of drinks and snacks while you rub shoulders with ski bums, seasonal residents, and other local artists and intelligentsia. But we come for the food.

You say tapas-style, I say small plates. There are so many advantages to this new wave of menu and meal service that Food Snob wants us to explain them all. For one, at very reasonable prices, you can sample and share with your friends a number of intriguing food combinations, and barVino excels in this category. Second, the plates are brought out as soon as they are prepared; no food sitting around losing quality under heat lamps, no bitter public recriminations between the front and back of the house about soggy French fries. Servers and chefs no longer have to coordinate the timing of plates for large parties. Lastly, the diner is more in charge, with increased influence on the pace and the volume of food, and expenditures can be moderated. Lesser appetites are just as easily accommodated as are voracious eaters looking to indulge after a day of skiing or hiking.

Regulars overwhelmingly swear by the gnocchi—made in-house fresh each day— and we tried a mushroom variety with brandy and bacon cream sauce. An outstanding effort, it left us wanting more, so why not, we ordered another plate. The mussels, a local favorite and a specialty of the house, arrived in a white wine, parsley, garlic and cilantro sauce. Food Snob proclaimed it a genuine Proustian moment, the mere smell transporting him into a long-winded rhapsody about moules et frites consumed on some long lost Parisian night. The fish taco two ways might have been our favorite dish, and the fresh-cut fries, sprinkled with sea-salt and Parmesan, were terrific. We can also endorse the steak frites, a worthy homage to French bistro fare. BarVino is definitely one of those places where every time a plate goes by, you crane your neck to see if just maybe you should have ordered that as well. Desserts are local as well, and feature choices from Café Sarah, another North Creek gem.

We've sent a number of people to barVino since our initial visit—picky foodies, beer snobs, wine lovers, working chefs, and demanding out-of-towners—and all have reported back favorably. BarVino is limited to about 25 seats at tables, and room for 17 at the bar. In season, this can entail a wait during peak hours, and reservations aren't taken. BarVino also features live music on Wednesdays from late April through September, and seats can get pretty scarce.

2. W.W. Durant (Raquette Lake, August 2011)

Docking in the village of Raquette Lake, just a short jaunt from The Tap Room (where many cruisers begin and end their evening's festivities) , the W.W. Durant has been family operated since 1991. Captain Dean Pohl pilots the ship and gives the historical narrative as the tour makes its way past some of the most famous Adirondack Great Camps, including the first one built by William Durant, Camp Pine Knot, as well as Echo Camp and the Carnegie's North Point Camp. Donna Pohl and daughter Rachel run the front of the boat, while son Jim heads the galley; the outgoing, hard-working family has naturally acquired the status of Raquette legends.

Although locals have been recommending the food on the W.W. Durant for some years, we confess to certain skepticism from one too many lousy boat experiences. After all, dinner cruises tend to be over-priced, and most travelers lower their expectations concerning the quality of the food, managing to focus more on the cocktails than the cuisine. An above average meal would generally be considered a success, and all too often the food quality resembles the "rubber chicken" or "dried out salmon with dill sauce" of banquet lore.

Run by friendly and passionate executive chef Jim Pohl for the last eight years, The W.W. Durant's dining experience is a definite exception to the norm, and is certainly worth taking the time and effort necessary to make a reservation. So here's the lowdown. You're going to need to call with a credit card and reserve a spot (and check the weather forecast, because the boat heads out rain or shine, and cancellations must be made 24 hours in advance). Two main dining options exist, with an "intimate" dining experience at $75 per person and the "traditional" service offered at $50 (gratuity included in either case), the difference being that reservations are more limited and no one under 18 is permitted on the higher end trip. The four-course meal is the same, and the tour is the same, so it is simply a matter of space. Other choices exist, such as cocktail and pizza cruises, so check the website or call for clarification, because it can be a tad confusing at first blush.

Because of limited galley space, your dinner choice must be pre-selected, generally from four or five options. Dinner begins with a soup course, in our case a light cream of broccoli, done with smoked Gouda cheese, an excellent touch which elevated the dish beyond the normal cheddar based versions. The salad was plentiful and the produce well-selected and chef's ginger dressing had a nice flair. We tried the prime rib, which was tender and correctly cooked, and definitely enhanced by the horseradish sauce served on the side; the Chilean sea bass, done with a innovative soy reduction with ligonberries, was fresh tasting and delicious, the fish being pan-seared perfectly. We all enjoyed the garlic smashed potatoes, which avoided the common sin of being overpowering and remained complementary to the dishes served. For dessert, all being homemade, we tried the cheesecake, which proved to be a light and airy treat, and not too rich after a sizeable meal.

Of note, during the winter months, the Durant is moored in the ice out in the middle of the lake and becomes a routine stop for many snowmobilers looking to warm up; then the menu is reduced to things like chili and hot dogs, and drinks are served in profusion.

All in all, the W.W. Durant serves better food than most of its land-based competitors, and Chef Jim Pohl takes great pride in his work, doing such extras as smoking meats and growing fresh herbs and seasonings. Locals also highly recommend the Sunday Brunch.

3. The Tap Room (Raquette Lake, October 2010)

Because the Tap Room is one of our favorite hole-in-the-wall bars in the world—too good to be true in many ways—we almost wanted to keep the place a native secret. Tucked away in the corner of an old brick building in the village of Raquette Lake, close to the town docks and the W.W. Durant, the Tap Room is popular with an eclectic mix of seasonal residents, camp counselors, and die hard locals.

Okay, so the Tap Room, despite its name, features only Yuengling Lager on draft, cheaply priced, and it tastes pretty good in the frosted mugs. But don't confine yourself to just drinking. The Tap Room is well-known for its homemade bar food, featuring excellent sandwiches (such as the grilled cheese with ham), good steamed clams, and is perhaps best known for its soup of the day (and we all agree that New England clam chowder is pretty good). The food is like stopping by that favorite relative's house, where for some reason ordinary food always tastes better than anywhere else. Insiders rave about Monday Pastabilities, where the regular menu is dismissed in favor of an all pasta line-up, with the linguine and clams being frequently mentioned as a salient favorite.

On our late night Saturday night visit, we found ourselves virtually alone at the bar until after the Durant returned to the dock, when suddenly the crowd surged in and things started hopping. Fueled by one of the better jukeboxes in the Adirondacks, where two dollars nets you nine songs from a selection of mostly classic rock, it doesn't take too many people singing before someone might start dancing on the bar. The place is so small that the overflow hangs outside smoking or drinking at the picnic tables.

If you're planning to get sloshed, we recommend booking one of the "no-frills" rooms upstairs to crash. The Adirondacks are known for tough enforcement, so really, don't drink and drive.

4. The Indian Lake Restaurant (Indian Lake, September 2010)

Head into the Indian Lake Restaurant on a chilly Friday night in the fall, and you might just find yourself having to wait for a table in this popular eating spot—in the summertime, the waiting list is just a standard part of the process. And while you wait, you might sort of scratch your head trying to figure out a word to describe the ambience (or anti-ambience in this case, not an uncommon problem for Adirondack restaurateurs, who often must concede to limited commercial real estate opportunities and a need to maintain low off-season overhead). Windowless, non-trendy, somewhat 70's Retro, this is so not the place for a romantic candlelit dinner—Food Snob couldn't help but quote Oscar Wilde's famous dying words, "Either the wallpaper goes, or I do." Having spent the day looking at the old-time photographs at the Adirondack Museum—the ones with the heavily bearded back-woodsmen and lumberjacks staring at you out of time—we got the distinct feeling that a few of those characters had snuck off from their pictures to grab a meal here (sort of like, for Woody Allen buffs, an Adirondack version of *The Purple Rose of Cairo*; we even thought about calling our friends at the museum to try to coax these guys back into their images). All in all, however, one is lead to an obvious conclusion about this place; these folks are here because the food is good and the prices are fantastic.

As almost all the local sources point out, the menu is huge. Being practically the only game in town, the Indian Lake Restaurant fulfills the need in the community to keep the regulars from getting bored and offers some diverse items to try to give the people what they want; tourists who stay near town will routinely eat here three or four times in a week. Food Snob, however, immediately expressed his conviction that this husband, John (chef), and wife, Ann (front of the house), operation couldn't possibly maintain quality control over so many different dish offerings. Happily, with a strong background in opening restaurants while working for a noted chain, he [John Miller] managed to defy expectations very well, and we're pretty happy he chose to open his own place here.

You're going to have a hard time deciding what to order, and, if you're anything like us, you'll be craning your neck trying to glimpse various dishes as they head to tables. Generally speaking, locals insist that you pretty much can't go wrong. Popular appetizers include the chicken and bean egg roll, nicely done. We sampled the Irish version of French onion soup, made with a Guinness enhanced broth, which came out very well; the stout complemented the caramelized onions with a bit more sweetness, while overall yielding great color, depth and heartiness to this slightly salty favorite. We also tried the New England clam chowder, which was, as the French like to say, "proper." The main courses yielded no complaints. The pasta hit the spot, the burgers and steaks were good, and the fries are definitely recommended, the chili had, on our visit, some wonderfully tender pieces of steak. About the only thing locals have been lukewarm about is the pizza.

Overall, we love this place. The good food easily trumps the glum ambience, and the economics of it really work for family vacations. There's a lot of local character interaction to be had for those looking to chat (check out the attached Tavern), and the owners are friendly, passionate and caring. And if, after several libations, you notice an occasional lumberjack who has wandered here from out of an old-time photograph, well, we can hardly blame him, and good luck trying to take him away until he's done with his plate.

5. The Hedges (Blue Mountain Lake, July 2010)

Dining at The Hedges is an evocative experience in both spirit and setting – you feel connected to the traditions of Adirondack summers past, when Blue Mountain Lake was an elite destination, and the place retains a rich ambience of a more leisurely way of life. Amidst historic buildings that reflect the Great Camp style of ornate rusticity, the restaurant itself features a Victorian era tin-tiled dining room with a fireplace and, at the far end, a fine view of Blue Mountain Lake. While the majority of diners are guests at The Hedges, non-guests are welcome via reservation, which, to be on the safe side, should be made a day or two in advance.

Since the primary focus of the restaurant is to cater to the on-site guests, the menu is small, offering three choices each night for the main entrée. Meals here come with soup, salad, main course and dessert, and all for the reasonable price of $25.00. Beverages are extra, and cocktails, beer and wine are available.

The night we sampled the fare, we started with a homemade Minestrone soup and then had a Greek salad served family-style with chilled salad plates (a nice touch). Our three entrees were all good, the pork tenderloin with apples and gravy, crab-stuffed flounder, and vegetarian pasta dish all being well-executed. Don't expect creative over-the-top "foodie" cuisine—this is not show-stopping stuff—but it is a delightful experience of simple dishes executed nicely.

Now, please be forewarned, they don't take credit cards, and we were spared considerable embarrassment after we emptied our pockets and were relieved to find we had enough on hand. With the usual jokes about doing the dishes, all in all, we had no idea where we would have found an ATM anywhere nearby.

After our meal, we looked over the room and cabin rates, and with each room including both dinner and breakfast for two, they seemed to be a remarkable value given the simple splendor of the lake front setting, and a comparable experience in, say, Lake Placid, might cost double. It is an excellent family vacation choice, and probably a fine romantic weekend, particularly after Labor Day.

We took one of our mothers with us for our evening here, and, after beaming for most of the meal, exclaimed that "I would definitely come back!"

6. The Adirondack Hotel (Long Lake, June 2011)

First, an admission and disclaimer before we begin this review: the staff members of this publication are predominately Long Lakers. No matter what we say here, it's very likely that an angry mob of villagers will show up at Food Snob's castle, with burning torches and all, and demand we give him over. And we're probably harder on our local restaurants than on any other locale, but, at the same time, these folks are our friends and neighbors, and we all want you to have a good time in our town.

Near the town bridge, the Adirondack Hotel has one of the premier locations in the North Country, with a spectacular view of the high peaks at the far end of the lake. The original structure, Kellog's Lake House, burned down in 1898, and the current structure dates, in part, from 1899. Just off the town beach, and across from Helm's Aero Service (where you can take a seaplane ride), the hotel has a rich history. Famous people who have visited this hotel include Helen Keller, Ann Sullivan, Rod Stewart, and Mick Jagger (see his picture across at Helm's, along with Spencer Tracy). Albert Einstein, who missed the Bavarian Alps and loved lake sailing, put up guests here. Yankee legend Mickey Mantle slept and probably drank profusely here in the 50's, taking the time to throw baseballs behind the building with the owner's grandson. An unverified local legend contends that Theodore Roosevelt once joined a mysterious woman for breakfast here, just days before becoming President (however, Food Snob notes, they don't serve breakfast anymore, so you'll have to take your mysterious women elsewhere).

The location means that it is often busy at dinner and lunch time, and, in season, can become quite chaotic. With such a short season here, so much is staked on turning tables in July and August that the food invariably becomes inconsistent. The Hotel's irresistible location makes it the hub of the town and, as insiders, we can tell you how to have a good experience here.

First of all, it's a great bar to hang out, and on nice days nothing beats sitting out on the rocking chairs on the front porch. Summer evenings can get a good young local crowd, and Friday nights with Chuck are a social tradition. Exchanging banter with Colleen can be a lot of fun as well; her conversational specialties are Bob Dylan and witty comebacks. When things have slowed down, and kindly Val is tending bar, she will take the time to make you a refreshing gin or vodka lemon fizz (Food Snob sometimes brings his own organic lemons, you should consider it). The chicken wings, onion rings, and pizza make good bar food, and the Kilcoyne Farm burgers are popular. On draft, the Switchback and Harpoon make good choices, and the ordinary domestics are laughably inexpensive.

For dining, reservations may help avoid a long wait on weekends like 4th of July, where large crowds gather for Long Lake's excellent fireworks show.

Food Snob has been appreciative of the hotel's new evening sous-chef, Darren, who handles the specials. Last year, the marinated tequila steak, the trout with citrus sauce, the blackened rib-eye and, for dessert, the passion fruit panna cotta were all dishes that would have passed muster at our highest rated restaurants. For families, Wednesday and Saturday barbecue nights are family favorites, as co-owner Carmine dons his chef's hat and apron to tend to the wood fire grill, but, as Food Snob notes, it's not for the fanatical Bobby Flay crowd.

The Adirondack Hotel has a unique collection of characters, from food critics, artists, museum workers, contractors, snowmobilers, hunters, fisherman, foreign visitors, Manhattanites, etc. It's also got a fine array of taxidermy, particularly the moose head and large bear in the lobby. If you want to get a sense of Long Lake, this is the place to rub shoulders and hang out. Large parties should reserve a table in the charming Victorian dining room— tin ceiling, antiques, overhead fans—it's good for an intimate seating as well.

Bar patrons, absent a designated driver, should book a room and enjoy some drinks.

7. Basil and Wick's (North Creek, May 2011)

We stopped in Friday night on a whim, gathering in the bar until we collected our team, while a trio of musicians covered various hits from the seventies. (Food Snob threatened to leave if they played CCR or the Doobie Brothers, but held to his seat because he had some Smuttynose). In a region where bartenders tend to hang with some local buddies while begrudgingly serving "outsiders," we felt unusually welcome, and no doubt appreciated the friendly banter as we chatted about the local North Creek scene.

In a something old, something new kind of way, the restaurant is located in the former Casey's North building, which stands on the site of the original Basil and Wick's, a legendary after skiing or rafting watering hole. The new place features a high vaulted ceiling, knotty pine beams, warm wine colored walls, and big windows that look out onto Route 28; the place is spacious and light. The décor is mostly a bit of kitsch, a sled here, skis there, a gigantic faux antler chandelier, a canoe—it's neither a plus or minus—but the old photographs of the original iteration are worth a look. One chair from the old restaurant is preserved and on display, a fine homage.

The foccacia bread served pre-meal was a highlight. We had the lobster roll as an appetizer, lots of mayonnaise on a grilled bun, and could almost have been a meal unto itself. The Friday night fish fry, a large portion bargain that included six scallops as well as the haddock, got the job done.

Without a doubt, however, Basil and Wick's will be known for one certain thing, and that's the hamburger. You've been told. If members of your party don't like hamburgers, take them somewhere else, or mock them while you complete this prime directive. The burgers themselves are a "build your own" process, and you select from a number of ingredients (which can add up; we modestly suggest that the menu include a few surefire combos in the future). These beauties are served on a lightly grilled freshly made Kaiser bun, the meat has terrific char-grilled flavor, and we want you to get the tobacco onions as one of your selections. The steak fries that come with the plate are wedge sized, and few can finish them all.

If you still have room, we recommend the homemade bread pudding which is easily enough for two to share.

8. The Lumberjack (Tupper Lake, January 2011)

Tupper Lake is a tough, hard scrapple Adirondack blue collar town. Hard working men depend upon big breakfasts to sustain them through the day, particularly in winter time.

Thus, the Lumberjack is exactly what you'd expect from its name. The décor: big pans, big saws, big axes. The food: big pancakes, huge portions of breakfast meats, gigantic pieces of toast, and large servings of eggs. Arguably the best breakfast in the central Adirondacks, the French toast is legendary.

Naturally, also in keeping with expectations, the prices are as cheap as sawdust.

9. Hemlock Hall (Blue Mountain Lake, July 2010)

Hemlock Hall makes for an interesting contrast with the Hedges. Travelers hooked on ideas of taking vacations at an old-fashioned Adirondack Resort—and on stunning Blue Mountain Lake in particular—should consider taking a meal at both of these places before deciding where to book. Before a day at the Adirondack Museum, dining here and taking a glimpse into a lost way of leisure can only enhance the coming day's experience.

The main building at Hemlock Hall is a treasure, with gleaming woodwork, cozy fireplaces, and comfortable nooks to read and relax. The elegant rusticity is completely compelling, and we found ourselves tempted to take one of the parlor games off the shelf and spend the day playing "Clue." You'll want to leave some time to wander around to get a full sense of this resort's charm.

We go here for breakfast, eight a.m. sharp. Call ahead, and make a reservation. It's family-style seating, so you get to mix with the guests—most will rave about their experiences at Hemlock, and you never know quite who you will meet. Many guests have been coming here summer after summer, and Hemlock is a deeply held attachment. Food Snob, a notorious grump in the morning, grew more impressed and loquacious with each cup of coffee.

Breakfast itself comes out on big platters to share camp-style, though eggs can be cooked to order. Ample portions of toast, pancakes, bacon, fresh baked bread, jelly—just the sort of food that's been served at Adirondack resorts in historic Blue Mountain for over 125 years—makes the rounds at the table. Good stuff, the meal is surprisingly inexpensive. Insiders also endorse the Wednesday night chicken and biscuits dinner.

10. The Cellar (Long Lake, June 2011).

The Cellar was originally started in a flat roofed, cinder block basement (no house ever got built) that outsiders sometimes referred to as "Bob's Country Bunker," a reference from the classic movie *The Blues Brothers*. Once a quintessential dive bar, where the floor tiles would stick to your feet, the Cellar's dingy pole dancing days are over. In the late 90's it was renovated into a "real" restaurant (but still lacks windows). On a hot, muggy summer's day, it's the only restaurant in Long Lake with true air-conditioning. This past winter, locals voted the Cellar "Best Hors d'oeuvres in Town" and The Cellar also holds third place in the Long Lake 4th of July Bed Races (where ridiculously costumed teams race beds on wheels down the streets of Long Lake).

The Cellar offers most of the standard Adirondack fare, everything from steaks and seafood to pizza and burgers. The pizza is a real kid-pleaser, doughy, good crust, we recommend the pepperoni as a topping. Their wings come with a peppery buffalo sauce, and their homemade chicken fingers are among our favorites; some people go to the Cellar just for their garlic bread. Now serving breakfast at 6:00 a.m., the local "round table" often gathers in the morning hours to discuss local and world events. The owner's Eggs Benedict are the best in town, with a homemade hollandaise sauce; this is the signature dish. The "Cellar Toast" also ranks.

The Cellar serves some interesting specials, and the fried jumbo shrimp and gyros will satisfy a craving. In the earlier dinner hours, an older crowd and families find the cuisine comforting and familiar. Ten till midnight the place can be crowded with residents and camp counselors. Late night, a fire-pit on the patio makes a great spot to have a pint, take in the night, and mingle as things thin out.

11. Quackenbush's Long View Wilderness Lodge (Long Lake, June 2011)

Locals continually refer to it as the Longview, despite new ownership and a modified moniker. Keeping in mind our Long Lake conflict of interest, this family run operation has an interesting background story. The father is a former Marine, and highly decorated Vietnam combat veteran (check out some of his medals and artifacts on display). Two of his sons, Justin and Jarod, are now operating the place, and are determined to make improvements from the last couple of years.

This historic hotel dates from 19th century, and it has a game parlor worth checking out. The knotty pine barroom has been remodeled, and possesses a fine view of the lake in the distance; the back deck isn't a bad place to take in the summer sunset or, as the natives do, have a draft while socializing.

Some of you recall the former Blarney Stone in town, which sadly burned to the ground a few years ago, taking down one of our favorite restaurants and hangouts. The former chef, Long Lake native Dustin Traynor, has recently signed onto the executive job here. Having worked on Beacon Hill before returning home, Dustin vows to ramp it up this July with a new dinner menu, and, for the first time in a long time, plans to offer lunch Friday through Sunday. For now, stick with the burgers, wings, Arancini (Italian fried rice balls, with cheese and tomato sauce), fried clams, French onion soup, Caesar salad, and, when available, Dustin's superb homemade ravioli with vodka sauce, or the in-house smoked trout appetizer.

Early local feedback has been encouraging, and the Long View appears committed to becoming one of the most improved restaurants in the area.

CENTRAL ADIRONDACK LOCAL LOWDOWN

Blue Mountain Lake

Blue Canoe Ice Cream

8814 Route 30
Blue Mountain Lake, NY 12812
(518) 352-9722
www.bluecanoeicecream.com

Local Lowdown: One of the only places to stop for a quick bite to eat or a bite to eat in Blue Mountain! .... "Good ice cream!"

The Hedges

Hedges Road
Blue Mountain Lake, NY 12812
(518) 352-7325
www.thehedges.com

Local Lowdown: Everything about it is a "class act" .... Limited menu, call for seating/reservations.... "Inn Keeper, Pat Benton, is great!" .... Traditional Adirondack experience with "sophistication."

Hemlock Hall

Maple Lodge Road
Blue Mountain Lake, NY 12812
(518) 352-7706
www.hemlockhall.com

Local Lowdown: Beautiful setting.... "Biscuits are delicious!" .... Good breakfast."

Lakeside Café at the Adirondack Museum

Route 30
Blue Mountain Lake, NY 12812
(518) 352-9722
www.adkmuseum.org/visiting/lake_view_cafe

Local Lowdown: They charge you the Adirondack Museum fee to get in, but you can get your money refunded on the way out if you're just eating.... "An unbelievable view!" .... "Good variety of sandwiches" .... "Get the BBQ pork sandwich" .... Kids corner.... "Make-your-own mac & cheese" .... Fresh salads and gluten free products.... Get the "Adirondack Snack Basket!" .... "Eat there just for the view!"

Childwold

Cranberry Lake Lodge

7202 New York Route 3
Clifton, NY 12927
(315) 848-3301
www.cranberrylakelodge.com

Local Lowdown: Popular snowmobile stop.... "Good place to warm up" .... "Nice, newly renovated rooms" .... "Good-sized portions."

The Thirsty Moose
9754 New York Route 3
Childwold, NY 12922
(518) 359-2540

Local Lowdown: "Owners from Jersey (Mickey very
funny)" .... Good seafood, pastas and burgers" .... "Good
place for snowmobilers and hunters to stop" .... Has gas for
snowmobilers.... "Unique horseshoe bar."

Indian Lake

The Bear Trap Inn
Main Street
Indian Lake, NY 12842
(518) 648-5341

Local Lowdown: "Late night bar of Indian Lake!" .... "Good
pizza, wings, burgers" .... Snowmobile to parking lot! .... "Very
tiny place" .... Open year-round.... "You may want to go in there
with the protection of a local."

Indian Lake Restaurant Inc.
2 East Main Street
Indian Lake, NY 12842
(518) 648-5115

Local Lowdown: "Gotta get the poutine (only in winter)!" ....
"French onion soup I still dream about!" .... "Big menu— lots
of choices" .... Dark on Wednesdays during the summer....
"Homemade meatloaf is good stuff" .... Closed in April.

Marty's Chili Nights

3 Main Street
Indian Lake, NY 12842
(518) 648-5832
www.chilinights.com

Local Lowdown: Serves dinner Thursday through Sunday....
"Good atmosphere!" .... Good margaritas.... "Can be pricey."

Long Lake

The Adirondack Hotel

1245 Main Street, Route 30N
Long Lake, NY 12847
(518) 624-4700
www.adirondackhotel.com

Local Lowdown: Families go for the BBQ on Wednesday
and Saturday nights.... "Good pizza" .... "Artichoke dip in
bread bowl is very popular!" .... "Fun night out" .... "Good
atmosphere" .... "Gets busy during summer season" .... They do
take reservations, but not required.

The Cellar Restaurant and Pub

3 Kickerville Road
Long Lake, NY 12847
(518) 624-5539
www.thecellarlonglake.com

Local Lowdown: Open for breakfast and dinner.... "Popular local
place" .... "Great garlic bread" .... Reservations recommended
(especially for large groups).... "Good pizza and sausage bread."

Custard's Last Stand

1 Lake Street
Long Lake, NY 12847
(518) 624-5371

Local Lowdown: "Best name ever" .... One of the oldest ice cream buildings in the Adirondacks! .... Made famous when the Long Lake Dump was open! Back then, travelers far and wide would travel to Long Lake to get ice cream and go to the dump to watch the bears! .... "Also known for their Michigan dog!" .... Under new ownership.... "Great soft ice cream" .... "Friendly service!"

Cyber Creek Café

8590 Newcomb Road #5
Long Lake, NY 12847
(518) 624-6466
www.cybercreekcafe.com

Local Lowdown: Check in with civilization while enjoying fresh homemade sandwiches (computers and Wi-Fi available).... "Panini's and homemade salads" .... Enjoy chatting with the owner, Phyllis, who grew up in the restaurant business.... "Good, fresh food" .... Serves breakfast, lunch, and special Italian dinners on select days.... Frequent Food Snob sightings at lunch.... Good baked goods.... Phyllis also does catering.

Hoss's Ice Cream Stand
1142 Main Street
Long Lake, NY 12847
(518) 624-2481
www.hossscountrycorner.com

Local Lowdown: On the corner of Route 28N and Route 30.... A small arcade and miniature golf next store.... The infamous Hoss's Country Corner Store across the street—with great gifts, books, meats and cheeses, camping supplies, and more.... The stand has "great ice cream" .... "You can get a quick lunch there" .... "Good sandwiches—hot corned-beef, sweet Italian sausage, and meatball subs" .... "I like the Gyro" .... "Try the Black Bear Sundae."

Long Lake Diner / Owl's Head Pub
(pub is in the back of the diner)
State Route 30
Long Lake, NY 12847
(518) 624-3941

Local Lowdown: "Love the early morning breakfast and the red-headed waitress who has been there for years!" .... Small, quaint bar in back known as "Owl's Head Pub" .... Diner is open for breakfast and lunch and has dinner specials Wednesday through Saturday during the summer season.... "The prime rib night and Friday night fish fry are good!"

Quackenbush's Long View Wilderness Lodge

681 Deerland Road
Long Lake, NY 12847
(518) 624-2862
www.quackenbushlongviewwildernesslodge.com

Local Lowdown: Formerly the Long View Lodge.... "Great atmosphere" .... Formal and informal dining rooms.... "Good chicken wings" .... Pool table .... Jukebox coming.... "Nice deck to sit and have a drink" .... "New chef this year—should be improved!"

Newcomb

Newcomb House
Route 28N
Newcomb, NY 12852
(518) 582-4401

Local Lowdown: The only bar in town.... "It's like walking into someone's living room" .... Snowmobiler stop in the winter.... Limited menu.... "Very local" .... "Fun times!"

North Creek

barVino
272 Main Street
North Creek, NY 12853
(518)251-0199
www.barvino.net

Local Lowdown: "Awesome food tapas-style!" .... "They prefer not to do take-out" .... "Good atmosphere—lots of wine and beer choices" .... "Fresh, fun food!" .... Family-run.... Closed Mondays.

The Barking Spider

302 Main Street
North Creek, NY 12853
(518) 251-9911

Local Lowdown: Fun bar at night.... Everybody loves the
owner/bartender, Tim.... Starting to serve burgers, clams, simple
but good bar food this June.... "Good-looking bartenders."

Basil & Wicks

Top 46

3195 Route 28
North Creek, NY 12853
(518) 251-3100
www.basilandwicks.com

Local Lowdown: Just opened up this 2011 ski season.... "Good
food!" .... Friday night fish fry.... "Burgers are awesome!" .... "Try
their homemade bread pudding!" .... "I like all the condiments
they have on the table!"

Black Mountain

2999 Route 8
North Creek, NY 12853
(518) 251-2800
www.blackmountainlodgeandrestaurant.com

Local Lowdown: Good portions! .... Packed every night, year-
round.... Have rooms you can stay at too! .... Get the calamari!

Café Sarah

260 Main Street
North Creek, NY 12853
(518) 251-5959

Local Lowdown: One word: pastries! .... Delicious coffee, espresso, cappuccino, lattés, sandwiches, and cookies! Homemade soups and salads.... Good breakfast and friendly atmosphere.... "One of best bakeries in Adirondack region" .... No credit cards.

Lorenzo's
307 Main Street
North Creek, NY 12853
(518) 251-2200
www.copperfieldinn.com/lorenzos.asp

Local Lowdown: "Excellent food" .... "Big supporters of the North Creek community and businesses" .... Not opening until July 1st 2011.... "The chef is outstanding" .... Will be reviewed in 2012 Adirondack Eats Edition.

Raquette Lake

Raquette Lake Tap Room & Hotel

Main Street
Raquette Lake, NY 13436
(315) 354-4581
www.raquettelaketaproom.com

Local Lowdown: Open seven days a week—all year long! .... "Quick and friendly service" .... "Good soup" .... Known for great (cheap) burgers, wings, and "pastabilities" .... "Dirt cheap" .... Veal parm, veal marsala, and clams fantastic; huge meatballs.... "Toasted cheese is so good!" .... "Good bar food" .... "Very short bar walk" (referring to dancing on top of bar).... "Always a great time."

Tony Harper's Clam & Pizza

459 Route 28
Raquette Lake, NY 13436
(315) 354-4222
www.tonyharperspizzaandclamshack.com

Local Lowdown: Two locations: Raquette Lake (seasonal) and in Old Forge (year-round).... "Get the ADK Whiskey Wings" .... "Good pizza" .... "Clams are amazing!"

W.W. Durant Boat

254 Antlers Road
Raquette Lake, NY 13436
(315) 354-5532
www.raquettelakenavigation.com

Local Lowdown: Lunch, dinner and Sunday brunch cruises.... "A class act" .... Family business since 1991. "Duck and tuna recommended" .... "Food is very good, place is very, very clean" .... "Service is professional." Reservations needed and credit card saves spot.... Winter boat serves as a bar/chili and soup stop for snowmobilers.... "One of a kind" .... "Among the best food in the Adk's" .... "Moonlight cruises are a lot of fun!" .... They also do private parties and special events.

Speculator

Logan's

Route 8
Speculator, NY 12164
(518) 548-3287
www.logans921.com

Local Lowdown: "Very homey feel" .... Bar and restaurant.... Kid-friendly.

Speculator Inn
Route 8
Speculator, NY 12164
(518) 548-3811
www.speculatorinn.com

Local Lowdown: "Good service, good food, moderately priced" .... Traditional food—prime rib and fish fry.... Homemade salad dressing—you can buy it by the bottle.... "Very homey dining room with fireplace" .... Also have bands and entertainment on special nights.

Melody Lodge
111 Old Indian Lake Road
Speculator, NY 12164
(518) 548-6562
http://melodylodge.com

Local Lowdown: "Best place to eat in Speculator" .... Formal dining room and light fare menus.... "Drinks can be a little pricey."

Tupper Lake

Lumberjack Inn

Top 46

76 Main Street
Tupper Lake, NY 12986
(518) 359-2910

Local Lowdown: "Awesome fresh cut fries and homemade bread" .... "Great French toast!" .... "It's a family tradition to go to breakfast here!" .... "Best breakfast place around" .... "Omelets are amazing, hash is fresh."

Mainstreet

79 Main Street
Tupper Lake, NY 12986
(518) 359-7449

Local Lowdown: Huge portions.... "Good traditional food" .... "In the junction" part of town by the railroad tracks.... "Good Ruebens" .... Serves breakfast, lunch, and dinner.

The Market Place

2494 Tupper-Saranac Highway
Tupper Lake, NY 12986
(518) 359-9500

Local Lowdown: On your way out of town toward Saranac Lake.... "Great sandwiches and salads, hot sandwiches too" .... Best subs in town."

Old Northern
12 Cliff Avenue
Tupper Lake, NY 12986
(518) 359-9833

Local Lowdown: "Local dive bar" .... "Busy at odd times/days of the week" .... Jukebox, pool table, and darts.... "A late-night hangout" .... Bathroom stall doors are shower curtains.... Live bands.

Skyline Ice Cream
1976 Route 30
Tupper Lake, NY 12986
(518) 359- 7288

Local Lowdown: "Best pistachio soft ice cream" .... "Broaster chicken superb" .... Large selection of ice cream! .... "Get the Fried Dough Sundae with anything you can think of on top."

Swiss Kitchen
92 Park Street
Tupper Lake, NY 12986
(518) 359-3513

Local Lowdown: On the main street going through Tupper.... "Best homemade pies" .... "Fresh turkey on turkey sandwiches" .... "Everyone goes there" .... Right next to the movie theatre.... "Best apple crumble in town!"

Trails End
41 Raquette River Drive, Route 30
Tupper Lake, NY 12986
(518) 359-7135

Local Lowdown: "A good biker bar" .... "Everyone knows 'Beard,' the owner" .... Open microphone nights" .... "Atmosphere with lots of character, think *Roadhouse* with Patrick Swayze" .... "Great Bloody Mary's" .... "Friendly/fun bartenders."

White Birch Café
218 Park Street
Tupper Lake, NY 12986
(518) 359-8044

Local Lowdown: Looks like an old barn converted into a restaurant.... "Good portions" .... "Great Delmonico Steak" .... "Best pizza in Tupper" .... Bloomin' onion is a staple.... "Good wings!"

Central Region

Adirondack Eats

WEST REGION:

Old Forge and Inlet

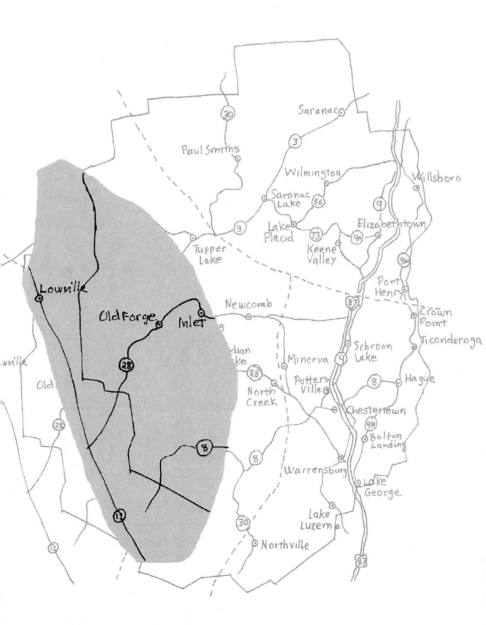

1. 5 Corners Café (Old Forge, May 2011)

This is the perfect place for Sunday brunch, and a lot of locals know it. Tucked into a small, narrow building near the main crossroads in Old Forge—diagonally across from the famous Hardware Store—don't be overly dismayed if there is a small line. They turn tables as efficiently as Evans to Tinker to Chance once turned the double play; it's sort of fascinating to see the serving staff's remarkable ability to communicate and help each other out, all the while exchanging pleasantries with the clientele. Despite the crowd, we noticed no signs of stress, and customers to all appearances seemed to be damned glad to be there. Outside seating is available as well.

In an area where the blueberry pancake stack once represented breakfast cuisine's apogee, the influence and acceptance of Mexican-style cooking on local menu offerings has been widely embraced. Come here, and it's mandatory that someone get the spicy chicken hash and eggs, a dramatic improvement on the fattening canned corned beef hash of so some many greasy spoons. The huevos rancheros also make a delicious choice. The more traditional fare that passed by also looked good. Not likely that you can go wrong on the breakfast menu, as well as the fresh-baked bread and muffins. In addition to the Five Corners Burrito, insiders champion the hamburgers as the best in town, and single out the key lime pie for special attention.

Now, temporarily, we have to rely on word of mouth for the following recommendation. Five Corners is open for dinner once a week (traditionally Mondays), and features a three-course set menu (two selections for each course) for $50. This event is so popular that several area residents have standing reservations in place for the entire summer and fall. We glanced over some of the menus, which highlight creative fare with international influences, like the Grouper filet with kiwi chutney and coconut milk, or the Moroccan-inspired crispy chicken with spices, lemon, green olives, and couscous. Hopefully, the kind blueberry cobbler can make a return appearance on our next much-anticipated visit.

2. Billy's Italian-American Restaurant (Old Forge, Nov. 2010)

It may not rise to the level of Montague versus Capulet, nor even to the rivalry of the wonderful film *Big Night*, but here in fair Old Forge, insiders are divided between two dueling houses of Italian-American cuisine, namely, Frankies' versus Billy's. It seems that Billy once worked for Frankie, and, as is natural in the restaurant business, Billy decided one day to strike out on his own, beginning operations about three years ago near the center of town in the backside of a small strip mall.

While Frankie's cavernous log-hewn restaurant at the edge of town has many seats and a widespread reputation, Billy has maybe 40 seats, not much of a view, and a building that has few advantages. If they would come, it wouldn't be for the décor, but for the food. Slowly, surely, word got out. To some, it was blasphemy, but more voices seemed to be suggesting that it was not Frankie's, but rather the upstart Billy's, who was now King of Italian in Old Forge.

Naturally, given the dramatic possibilities, our intrepid review team set out to investigate. Our first foray came on Columbus Day weekend, where, arriving mid-evening on a Saturday night, we were turned away for want of a reservation. Naturally, we were impressed—it shows a commitment to quality control and good pacing in the kitchen. With that lesson learned, we returned a few weeks later with one in hand, set at 6:30, and we saw that, not long after we were promptly seated, that the house was going to be fully-booked. So plan ahead, it's not an easy table to get.

We noted some menu similarities between the two. Is a rigatoni by any another name still a ridge-lined tube shaped pasta? Evidently yes, for at both places they are called Riggies, and are a popular dish. However, we chose to start our meal with an eggplant appetizer, thinly sliced and crisp, served in a lemon butter sauce, which impressed (the only Food Snob knock being that it was a tad oily). The portion was gigantic, easily enough for four, and a bargain at the price. The salad was fine, served with a house vinaigrette that thankfully lacked balsamic over-sweetness. The eggplant *parmigiana*, with ricotta, mozzarella and provolone, came out nearly perfect. The marinara had great depth and flavor, the eggplant was thin and crisp, and the combination of cheeses nicely complimentary, none calling out for exclusion (Our Food Snob waxed about it being nearly as good as the best eggplant he'd ever eaten, one night in Mantua, Italy). The haddock francese met with a bit more of a mixed reception. One of us, (can you guess?) thought that, given that the "house specialty" tag, the batter was rich, with too much egg taste, while the rest of us enjoyed the lemon sauce and didn't agree with our dear friend.

All in all, we like Billy's hearty portions, mid-scale prices, and good food. You probably can't go wrong with anything that has the marinara, and many other dishes looked interesting as they passed us by. Overall, Billy's seems very committed to making sure you have a pleasant dining experience, and the food and service reflects this well.

3. Seventh Lake House (Inlet, June 2010)

Long a dependable dining choice in a region known for inconsistency, chef Jim Holt and wife Chris have been guiding this family business since 1989. Over the years, our staff has eaten there on many occasions, without a single disappointing dining experience, whether it was a large special event to a quiet couples night.

Located on Route 28 with a direct view of the water, the Seventh Lake House opens its enclosed back porch seating during the summer season, and out back makes a great casual place to eat. In the colder months, the stone fireplace, rustic wood beams, wine racks, and white tablecloths give the place a cozy warm feel on dark fall and winter nights.

The menu is interesting, in that the appetizers tend to be more eclectic, a lot of Asian influences, while the entrees are more traditional. We started with the Won Ton Shrimp, paper-wrapped and served with mango marinade and crab cakes with basil tartar sauce—both were a success. We also had the"House Smoked Rainbow Trout Filet" which just seems to belong on an Adirondack menu.

Everybody, including the New York Times Travel Section, raves about the "Triple Meatloaf." A combination of wonderfully seasoned veal, pork, and beef—served in a pastry shell with a sherry-onion sauce—this signature dish takes a traditional comfort food and elevates it into something transcendent, and all for just $15.00. Another noted dish is the "Cowboy" steak, a spice-rubbed, pan-seared rib-eye served with *au jus*, a Food Snob preferred selection. The shrimp "Zydeco," a Cajun inspired pasta dish, has been mentioned by several locals as one of their favorites.

Seventh Lake House serves dinner every night in season; reservations are strongly advised.

4. Knotty Pine (Thendara, March 2011)

The Knotty Pine, in true Retro fashion, has hardly changed in appearance in over 50 years. The white exterior and green shutters still give the place the appearance of a house rather than a restaurant, and the signature knotty pine interior invokes memories for regulars who have been dining there for years. The parking lot gets crowded, and, interestingly, we can confirm that even some of the leading food critics in the Adirondacks have been sent packing on a weekend when arriving without reservations.

One of Food Snob's favorite recollections as a kid was getting the homemade applesauce and whipped butter with the bread at the beginning of the meal, a wonderful tradition that continues. The French onion soup makes a good starter. Locals recommend the specials, and we've enjoyed the Beef Wellington, not often seen on area menus, which makes a good choice for beef and mushroom lovers. On our recent visit, we ordered the steak *au poivre*, which came out tender, cooked perfectly to order, and with an excellent brandy and peppercorn sauce.

Locals recommend the homemade desserts, including the chocolate covered strawberries and chocolate mousse. We couldn't resist having the Bananas Foster, but note that this is not a theatrical table-side event, but comes out of the kitchen. Service has also been quite good.

The Knotty Pine continues to serve really good traditional Adirondack fare. Foodies may be miffed by a lack of innovation and vegetarian options, but regulars know that you come here for the well-prepared steaks or chops.

5. Frankie's Taste of Italy (Old Forge, August 2010)

From the outside, Frankie's Taste of Italy is the kind of place that you might pass by in favor of some of the more centrally located venues in Old Forge. The sign outside says "fuggedaboutit" under the name of the restaurant, and that sort of thing did nothing to buoy the expectations of Food Snob, who began whining that he couldn't eat anyplace with that sort of "subtitle." However, numerous—and we mean numerous—glowing local recommendations made this a must try, and the reasonable members of the team dragged him inside.

Frank Sinatra was playing when we walked in (more groans from the F.S.), and the pleasant knotty pine interior gave more of a Northern Italian/Adirondack ambience than something Sicilian. Onward, perhaps the rest of the meal would meet its billing.

Next up, another Italian restaurant litmus test, too bad that the bread, despite being hot and crisp, was not extraordinary by any stretch, and there was no olive oil to dip it in, just packets of ordinary butter, and it tasted like something from the supermarket. The salad came in a big bowl to be distributed at the table family style; the house balsamic dressing was fine and the salad produce crisp; overall, it lacked anything memorable about it like some great croutons or superior tomatoes. The sampler plates we tried featured meatballs, one piece of Frankie's homemade sausage, two raviolis, and some ziti cooked properly *al dente*. Regrettably, the manicotti and ravioli were overdone and lacked texture, and since both were stuffed with ricotta, no opportunity for a taste contrast occurred. The marinara sauce, despite a watery consistency (from failing to drain the pasta properly), had great depth to the flavor; one of us was tempted to finish off the sauce with a spoon. The sausage and meatball were both well seasoned and really stood out—knowing that the sausage was so good should lend confidence to your selection of dishes such as Annies' Riggies, which features the sausage in a cream sauce, which several insiders strongly recommended as the finest dish on the menu.

For dessert, well, the gelato is superb, homemade with ingredients shipped from Italy, and it is a stand out. One very cool touch was that the gelato cart, inside the front door, where samples were handed out to both kids and Food Snob alike, allows each diner to make an educated selection after trying a few of the many flavors.

We noted that several families sauntered in over the course of our meal, fresh from a hyper-active day at the Old Forge water park; Frankie's is definitely strong on family comfort, with spacious tables, prompt service, a tolerant attitude, etc. Large parties should find it easier to be accommodated here rather than many of the smaller Old Forge dining venues, a real plus.

Managing expectations is probably a good idea before eating here, and the gushing praise we'd heard might have raised the bar too high for our first visit. Maybe it was the five o'clock arrival, as things definitely improved over the course of the meal. Therefore, you'll probably find that the main dishes are good enough to make for an enjoyable and reasonably priced meal.

6. The Screamen' Eagle (Inlet, August 2010)

Viewed from Route 28 as you make your way through the visitor packed downtown of Inlet in the summer, the Screamen' Eagle looks like a fairly undistinguished local pizzeria. As you make your way through the front door, the layout is confusing enough that you might almost turn around in despair—is this a video store (actually yes)? What's with the cafeteria-style ordering system for the dining room? And where are the homemade pies we've heard about?

Here, a little persistence will pay off, so keep heading for the back of the joint, where you eventually can choose between the bar or, weather permitting, the large outdoor deck that features a charming view of the canal. If you're a sports fan, you'll appreciate the three high resolution flat screen televisions by the bar, and, a word to the wise, it's probably best not to bad mouth Ohio State or Cleveland at this family run operation, now in its twentieth year.

We admit to being biased in favor of a restaurant that knows what it's about, and, as the local clientele and seasonal regulars will proudly tell you, the Screamen' Eagle is about pizza, wings and beer. The wings are crisp and clean, and come in over fifteen different sauces, from the traditional Buffalo styles to creative entrees such as the "Peanut Butter Panic", a selection that proved tasty and was not overwhelmed with sticky sweetness as we feared it might be. The pizzas, frankly, do not look as good as they taste, so again, persist. We tried the taco-style pizza, something that would normally cause Food Snob considerable reticence before ordering, and all of us were pleasantly surprised by the texture of the medium thick crust and the ample toppings.

Beer lovers will especially appreciate the selection of over twenty beers on tap, all incredibly low priced, and featuring an array of American microbrews and a handful of interesting imports. Our bartender, initially a bit reserved, was all too glad to help us make an informed choice, and sampling different beers, chatting with the friendly seasonal and local clientele—and all this on a temperate August evening—well, needless to say, we had a good time.

Don't forget to save room for a slice of pie, only available in July and August.

WESTERN ADIRONDACK LOCAL LOWDOWN

Eagle Bay/Big Moose

Big Moose Inn
1510 Big Moose Road
Eagle Bay, NY 13331
(315) 257-2042
www.bigmooseinn.com

Local Lowdown: Serves lunch and dinner.... "Newer owners in last three years" .... Fun place to fly into by seaplane.... (Or drive to).... "Good place for weddings and other functions" .... Reservations recommended.

Big Moose Station
2138 Big Moose Road
Eagle Bay, NY 13331
(315) 357-3525
www.bigmoosestation.com

Local Lowdown: "Go for the king crab legs—Sunday" .... Serves breakfast, lunch, and dinner.... Reservations are appreciated.... Located "way back on Big Moose Road" (about seven miles).

Daiker's

161 Daikers Circle
Old Forge, NY 13420
(315) 369-6954
www.daikers.com

Local Lowdown: Serves lunch and dinner—view of 4th Lake....
"Really fun bar—wild" .... Ping-pong, video games, and pool
table.... Great for snowmobilers.... "Wood stove is awesome!" ....
Full menu, mud wrestling.... "Good fish fry" .... Outdoor deck....
"Love that bar!"

Eagle's Nest Motor Inn

5496 Route 28
Eagle Bay, NY 13331
(315) 357-3898

Local Lowdown: "Best fish fry hands down!" .... "Prices are
great.... You won't be disappointed."

The Glenmore Bar & Grill

146 Glenmore Road
Eagle Bay, NY 13331
(315) 357-4891
www.glenmorebarandgrill.com

Local Lowdown: Located "six miles north of Eagle Bay on
Big Moose" .... "A great place if you can find it" .... Welcomes
snowmobilers.... Serves late-night food every night.... Known for
their "comfort food" .... "Family place" .... Do not accept credit
cards, but have an ATM.... "You can get a room and stay over!"

Hard Times Café

5521 County Route 28
Eagle Bay, NY 13331
(315) 357-5199

Local Lowdown: Special Mexican nights.... "Not good bar/food
service at the bar, sit at a table."

Norridgewock

150 Norridgewock Lake Road, Beaver River
Eagle Bay, NY 13331
(315) 376-6200
www.beaverriver.com

Local Lowdown: "This place makes its own power!" .... Open
year-round.... "Great to snowmobile to in the winter!" .... On the
way to Stillwater Reservoir, half-way between Sabattis Circle and
Eagle Bay, on the tracks Sabattis Trail South.... Can only get to by
train tracks, boat or snowmobile.... "Fun just trying to find this
place!".... Tavern, restaurant, and a place to stay.... "Flashlights
are a must!" .... They have a "Riverboat Wilderness Cruise" that
leaves Stillwater twice a day in summer season!

The Tavern
Route 28
Eagle Bay, NY 13331
(315) 357-4305

Local Lowdown: "It may look closed in the day, but check closely" .... There is no menu here—but they are famous for the $2.00 "Larry Burger"—you get a freshly-ground burger on a toasted bun, with standard chips and pickle, as long as you go before 6:30 p.m.... Onions & hot peppers can be added too! .... "Beers are outrageously cheap" .... "Good snowmobile stop!" .... Bathrooms labeled "pointers" and "setters" .... Pool table and picnic tables to sit at inside the bar.

Wayback Inn
1910 Big Moose Road
Eagle Bay, NY 13331-2306
(315) 357-6000

Local Lowdown: "Way, way, way back there" .... "Great snowmobiling stop" .... "Awesome local, in-season place to go" .... "Cheers" place of the backwoods.... "Great nightly specials!" .... Closes at midnight.

Inlet

Drake's
363 Route 28
PO Box 268
Inlet, NY 13360
(315) 357-5181

Local Lowdown: Serves breakfast, lunch and dinner.... "Family place" .... "Good sandwiches" .... Try the "Fried Egg Burger" .... "Simple, but good" .... "Great fish fry."

Mary's White Pine Bakery
152 Route 28
PO Box 268
Inlet, NY 13360
(315) 357-5170

Local Lowdown: Open year-round.... "Good bagels, bread, and pastries."

The Ole Barn
74 Limekiln Road
PO Box 255
Inlet, NY 13360
(315) 357-4000
www.TheOleBarn.com

Local Lowdown: Big snowmobiler stop—they sell gas.... Serves lunch and dinner year-round.... Homemade soups, wings, and pizza.... Big menu/bar.... "Gets hectic, so sometimes the service is not the best."

Northern Lights Ice Cream
162 Route 28
Inlet, NY 13360
(315) 357-6294

Local Lowdown: Gelato ice cream made there.... Lots of different kinds of ice cream: Amaretto, Blue Moon, Guinness flavors, etc.... "Really good."

Tammarack Café & Movie House
153 Route 28
Inlet, NY 13360
(315) 357-2001

Local Lowdown: "Good portions" .... "Mmm, blueberry pancakes" .... "Good for breakfast" .... Attached to the movie theatre in Inlet.

Red Dog Tavern
2862 South Shore Road
Inlet, NY 13360
(315) 357-5502
www.reddogtavern.com

Local Lowdown: Famous for their wings—Armagedon Wing sauce—"unbelievably hot!" .... (One of our tasters requested milk immediately upon consuming!).... "Good nacho platter, Friday night fish fry"

Screamen Eagle / Matt's Draft House
172 Route 28
Inlet, NY 13360
(315) 357-6026
www.mattsdrafthouse.com
www.scrameneaglepizza.com

Local Lowdown: Looks like a video store—because you can also rent DVD's here too! .... Fresh pies, chicken wings, and pizza.... "Good after hiking" .... Outside seating on deck.... Twenty beers on tap.... "Good wine selection" .... "Try the peanut butter wings."

Top 46

Seventh Lake House Restaurant
479 Route 28
Inlet, NY 13360
(315) 357-6028
www.sevethlakehouse.com

Local Lowdown: "Great family restaurant" .... "Consistent good food" .... "Upscale" .... "Quality and great service."

The Woods Inn
148 Route 28
Inlet, NY 13360
(315) 357-5300
www.thewoodsinn.com

Local Lowdown: On Fourth Lake in downtown Inlet....
"Beautiful place right on the lake!" .... "Ghost activity there" ....
"Good lunches, you can boat there too!" .... "Nice bar and great formal dining too" .... "Good for weddings and functions—beautiful rooms!"

Lowville

Stillwater
2591 Stillwater Road
Lowville, NY 13367
(315) 376-6470
www.stillwateradirondacks.com

Local Lowdown: Located on Stillwater Reservoir—Marian and Joe Romano are your hosts and Joe "is quite a joke teller" ....
"Good bread" .... "It's way out there past Big Moose" .... "Excellent filets" .... "Get the Surf & Turf" .... Unique dining and lodging.

Pine Tree Tavern
Brantingham Road
Brantingham, NY 13312
(315) 348-6040
www.snowmobilingusa.com/Pine_Tree_Inn.htm

Local Lowdown: "Fun, food, cocktails, music, and dancing" ....
"Best time to go is during snowmobiling season!" .... "Fun winter
carnival" ....They sell gas too!

Old Forge/ Thendara

Adirondack Pizzeria
Main Street
Old Forge, NY 13420
(315) 369-6028

Local Lowdown: "Love the pizza" .... "Largest arcade and
pizzeria in the Adirondacks!" .... You can eat inside, outside, or
take out.... Ice cream too!

Benny's Ice Cream
2933 State Route 28
Old Forge, NY 13420
(315) 369-6636
www.bennysicecream.com

Local Lowdown: Next to Nutty Putty miniature golf.... "Good ice
cream" .... Home of "Mister Twister" and "Mister Twister's Sister."

Billy's Italian-American Restaurant

Route 28
Old Forge, NY 13420
(315) 369-2001

Local Lowdown: Located behind Walt's Diner.... "Former cook from Frankie's" .... Some claim "sauce is better here than at Frankie's" .... "Small, you need reservations during busy seasons" .... Owner has been "extremely generous in supporting community events."

5 Corners Café

3067 Route 28
Old Forge, NY 13420
(315) 369-2255

Local Lowdown: Wooden building across from hardware store.... Serves breakfast and lunch.... Summer Monday night dinners—a couple of options to choose for dinner.... "Best food in Old Forge!" .... "Bread is baked daily at the restaurant" .... "If you are someone who likes to cook with local, organic, wholesome, fresh ingredients then this is the one of the few places you will find in the Old Forge/Inlet area."

Frankie's Taste of Italy

2824 Route 28
Old Forge, NY 13420
(315) 369-2400
www.frankiesitalianfood.com

Local Lowdown: "Best Italian food in the area!" .... "Excellent gelato!" .... "Frankie has a big following" .... "Wait may be forever, but it's worth it!"

Keyes Pancake House & Restaurant

2967 Route 28
Old Forge, NY 13420
(315) 369-6752
www.KeyesPancakeHouse.com

Local Lowdown: Breakfast served all day.... Lots of different syrup flavors.... Very family-friendly.

Knotty Pine Restaurant

2776 Route 28
Thendara, NY 13472
(315) 369-6859
www.theknottypine.com

Local Lowdown: "Soooo homey!" .... Bread served with butter and applesauce! .... "Nice selection of wines" .... "Good traditional food" .... Operating for over seventy-five years!

The Old Mill Restaurant

2888 Route 28
Old Forge, NY 13420
(315) 369-3662
www.oldmilloldforge.com

Local Lowdown: "Everything is fresh tasting" .... "Great specials" .... Known for their family-style soup and salad.... "Reasonable prices and good people there" .... "Very popular and well-known."

Pied Piper
Route 28
Old Forge, NY 13420
(315) 369-3115

Local Lowdown: A "drive-in" .... "Good ice cream stop" .... You can drive or boat to it! .... "Hot dogs and broasted chicken" .... "A family tradition."

Seasons Adirondack Café
12228 Route 28
Woodgate, NY 12494
(315) 392-6556

Local Lowdown: Casual diner.... Open daily for breakfast and lunch.... "Best breakfast around" .... Friday night fish fry and Saturday night prime rib.... On snowmobile trail.

Sisters Bistro
3046 Route 28
Old Forge, NY 13420
 (315) 369-1053
www.sistersbistro.com

Local Lowdown: "Totally different from anything else" .... "Beautiful place" .... "Good for appetizers" .... "Entrees are small, expensive, but delicious" .... "Classy, cool, excellent wine" .... Menu is made with "fresh and local ingredients" ....To be reviewed 2012.

Slickers Adirondack Tavern

3132 Route 28
Old Forge, NY
(315) 369-3002
www.slickerstavern.com

Local Lowdown: "Great mushroom burgers, good portions" ....
"A fun night out!" .... Snowmobilers welcomed.... "You can boat
to it too."

Van Auken's

108 Forge Street
Thendara, NY 13472
(315) 369-3033
www.vanaukensinne.com

Local Lowdown: Open year-round.... Serving lunch and
dinner.... Thursday night is "Seafood Night"—very popular....
Neat, old hotel across from the train station.... Reservations
recommended for Friday and Saturday nights.

Walt's Diner

3047 Main Street
Old Forge NY 13420
315-369-2582

Local Lowdown: Open from 6 a.m. until 8 p.m. in the summer....
For breakfast "try the fresh oatmeal or the delicious blueberry
pancakes" .... "One of the better burgers in town" .... "The chili
hits the spot" .... "Fridays try the fresh fried haddock."

White Lake Inn

12678 Route 28
Woodgate, NY 12494
(315) 392-5439

Local Lowdown: South of Old Forge.... "Go for the prime rib."

Adirondack Eats

FAVORITE LISTS:

The Top 46 & Best of's

Top 46

1. **Farmhouse on Top of the World**, Lake George
2. **barVino**, North Creek
3. **Grist Mill**, Warrensburg
4. **Liquids & Solids**, Lake Placid
5. **Chair Six**, Lake Placid
6. **Café Adirondack**, Pottersville
7. **5 Corners Café**, Old Forge
8. **Caffé Rustica**, Lake Placid
9. **Caribbean Cowboy**, Lake Placid
10. **Lisa G's**, Lake Placid
11. **W.W. Durant**, Raquette Lake
12 **Friends Lake Inn**, Chestertown
13. **Brown Dog Café**, Lake Placid
14. **Raquette Lake Tap Room**, Raquette Lake
15. **Noon Mark Diner**, Keene Valley
16. **Eat & Meet Grill**, Saranac Lake
17. **Brunettos**, Warrensburg
18. **Hague Firehouse**, Hague
19. **Billy's Italian-American**, Old Forge
20. **7ᵗʰ Lake House**, Inlet
21. **The Indian Lake Restaurant**, Indian Lake
22. **The Hedges**, Blue Mountain Lake
23. **George's Place for Steak**, Lake George
24. **Knotty Pine**, Old Forge
25. **Frankies' Taste of Italy**, Old Forge
26. **Lake View Deli**, Saranac Lake
27. **Simply Gourmet**, Lake Placid
28. **Café Vero**, Lake George
29. **The Cottage**, Lake Placid
30. **Screamen Eagle**, Inlet

31. **Jimmy 21's**, Lake Placid
32. **The Adirondack Hotel**, Long Lake
33. **Basil & Wicks**, North Creek
34. **Lake Placid Pub & Brewery**, Lake Placid
35. **The Barnsider**, Lake George
36. **The Belvedere**, Saranac Lake
37. **The Lumberjack Inn**, Tupper Lake
38. **Pan Dolce**, Lake Placid
39. **Hemlock Hall**, Blue Mountain Lake
40. **The Place**, Chestertown
41. **The Cellar**, Long Lake
42. **Fredericks**, Bolton Landing
43. **The Loft**, Lake George
44. **Quackenbush's Long View Lodge**, Long Lake
45. **Anywhere's a Better Place to Be**, Chestertown
46. **Red Fox**, Saranac Lake

Best Bakeries
1. Café Sarah, North Creek
2. Gunnison Orchards, Crown Point
3. Noon Mark Diner, Keene Valley
4. Pan Dolce, Lake Placid
5. Little Nony's Bakery, Minerva

Best Breakfast Places
1. 5 Corners, Old Forge
2. Noon Mark Diner, Keene Valley
3, Caffé Vero, Lake George
4. The Lumberjack, Tupper Lake
5. Blue Moon Café, Saranac Lake
6. Chair Six, Lake Placid
7. The Swiss Kitchen, Tupper Lake
8. Hometown, Bolton Landing
9. Jingles, Saranac
10. Wagon Wheel, Ticonderoga

Best Deli Sandwiches
1. Lake View Deli, Saranac Lake
2. Simply Gourmet, Lake Placid
3. Saranac Sourdough, Lake Placid
4. Jacob & Tony's, Warrensburg
5. Cyber Creek Café, Long Lake

Best Beer on Tap
1. Screamen Eagle, Inlet
2. Bar Vino, North Creek
3. Liquids & Solids, Lake Placid
4. Lake Placid Pub & Brewery, Lake Placid
5. Steak & Seafood, Lake Placid

Best Burgers
1. Liquids & Solids, Lake Placid
2. Basil & Wicks, North Creek
3. Lisa G's, Lake Placid
4. Lake Placid Pub and Brewery, Lake Placid
5. Suzie Q's, Brant Lake
6. Anywhere's a Better Place to Be, Chestertown
7. The Loft, Lake George

Best Desserts
1. Grist Mill, Warrensburg
2. Liquids & Solids, Lake Placid
3. Noonmark Diner, Keene Valley
4. Pan Dolce, Lake Placid
5. Café Adirondack, Pottersville
6. Sisters Bistro, Old Forge
7. Screamen Eagle, Inlet

Best Ice Cream
1. Donnelly's Ice Cream, Saranac Lake
2. Martha's, Lake George
3. Northern Lights Ice Cream, Inlet
4. Benny's Ice Cream, Old Forge
5. Wind-Chill Factory, Ticonderoga
6. Main Street Ice Cream Parlor, Chestertown
7. Skyline Ice Cream, Tupper Lake
8. Custard's Last Stand, Long Lake

Best Places to Watch Sports
1. Lake Placid Pub and Brewery, Lake Placid
2. Screamen Eagle, Inlet
3. Basil and Wick's, North Creek
4. Dancing Bears, Lake Placid

Best Chicken Wings

1. Lisa G's, Lake Placid
2. Screamen Eagle, Inlet
3. Duffy's, Lake George
4. Red Dog Tavern, Inlet
5. Long View Lodge, Long Lake
6. Daikers, Eagle Bay
7. Fredericks, Bolton Landing
8. The Cellar, Long Lake
9. Adirondack Hotel, Long Lake
10. Fort View Inn, Ticonderoga

Date Nights (not ranked)
The Grist Mill, Warrensburg
The Cottage, Lake Placid
The Hedges, Blue Mountain Lake
Farmhouse on Top of the World, Lake George
Café Adirondack, Pottersville
WW Durant- (single table night), Raquette Lake
Brown Dog Café, Lake Placid
Mirror Lake Inn, Lake Placid
Lake Placid Lodge, Lake Placid
Interlaken Inn, Lake Placid
Melody Lodge, Speculator

Party Nights (not ranked)
The Adirondack Hotel, Long Lake
BarVino, Northcreek
The Bear Trap, Indian Lake
Black Bear, Pottersville
Charlies Inn, Lake Clear
Daikers, Eagle Bay
Duffy's, Lake George
George Henry's, Warrensburg
Tap Room, Raquette Lake
Rumors, Lake Placid
Slickers, Old Forge
Sporty's, Minerva
Trails End, Tupper Lake
Way Back Inn, Eagle Bay
The Waterhole, Saranac Lake
Zig Zags, Lake Placid

Best Places for Snowmobiling

"Snowmobilers like a place that is easy to get to, near where they can get gas, and has beer, burgers, fries, and French onion soup."
— Colleen Smith, Adirondack Bartender

North Area
The Shamrock, Saranac Lake
Gaga's, Bloomingdale
Charlies Inn, Lake Clear

Central:
The Tap Room, Raquette Lake
WW Durant "Winter Boat", Raquette Lake
The Adirondack Hotel, Long Lake
Long Lake Diner, Long Lake
The Newcomb House, Newcomb
The Bear Trap, Indian Lake
The Thirsty Moose, Childwold
Cranberry Lake Lodge, Cranberry Lake

West Area
Daiker's, Old Forge
Slickers, Old Forge
Tow Bar Inn, Old Forge
Norwich Walk—on way to Stillwater Reservoir
Stillwater Hotel, Lowville
Pine Tree Inn, Brantingham
The Glenmore Bar & Grill, Eagle Bay
Big Moose Inn, Big Moose
The Wayback Inn, Big Moose
The Ole Barn, Inlet
Red Dog Tavern, Inlet
Seventh Lake House, Inlet

Best Nights Out in Saratoga, NY (not ranked)

Cantina
www.cantinasaratoga.com
 On the main drag in Saratoga.... "Love the homemade chips and salsa at the bar"...."Good dinner food" .... "Good to go on dates here."

Circus Circus
http://circuscafe.com
"Fun.... They have good chocolate Martinis and fun desserts (cotton candy)" .... "Good kid menu" .... Karyoke and open microphone nights.

Dangos
"Good, newer place, right on Caroline" .... Known for their 5-cent wing night on Tuesday nights.... "Good burgers and wraps too" .... "Great for wings and beers."

Gotcha's
On Beekman Street on the West side of Saratoga.... "Homemade pasta!" .... "Good variety of beers on draft and delicious appetizers" .... "Try the Gotchya Balls!"

Hatties
www.hattiesrestaurant.com
Southern cuisine.... "I love their chicken wings" .... "Sal the bartender in the back/outside bar is fun to sit with."

Irish Times

http://irishtimessaratoga.com
Good place to hang out for happy hour (stops at 7pm).

The Local

www.thelocalpubandteahouse.com
On the West side of Saratoga.... "Good food and beers" ....
"Great appetizers!"....They have a "mug club" too.

9 Maple

http://9mapleavenue.com
"Very posh" .... Large variety of scotches and fine liquor....
"Delicious martinis—white chocolate or espresso martinis are to
die for!" .... Nice to go to after the track—sometimes big winners
at the track buy everyone drinks there!"

The Parting Glass

www.partingglasspub.com
Another Irish place (the original in Saratoga) .... "Good
sandwiches and wings" .... "Cider on tap" .... Dart boards in back
bar area.... "They have good bands (lots of Irish bands)."

The Stadium

www.thestadiumcafe.com
Two locations, one on main street the other on the West Side....
"Good calamari" .... "Great place to watch sports!"

Sassy Waitress Snappy Answers to Frequent Questions

As compiled by Molly Irvine.

Question: "Is the Haddock from the lake here?"
Snappy answer: "Of course."

Truth: Haddock is a saltwater fish. We have fresh water in our lakes here in the Adirondack Park.

Question: "Is the seafood fresh?"
Snappy answer: "Yes, flown in daily."

Truth: Not likely, as in order to get up to the Adirondacks nearly all seafood has to be frozen at some point, whether on the boat, or in transit the 200 miles to get here

Question: "Can we move the tables so that all seventeen of us can sit together?"
Snappy answer. "No."

Truth: Although we are in the woods, we still have fire codes.

Question: "Is the trout fresh from the lake?" Or, "Did you guys shoot the venison?"
Snappy answer: "Sure."

Truth: No. Regulations prevent this sort of freshness.

Question: "Is there any butter or oil in this?"
Snappy answer: "Of course there is.... That's how you make things taste good."

Truth: Of course there is.

Comment: "I'm allergic to mushrooms and garlic."
Snappy answer: "Right. No problem."

Truth: They don't believe you; think you are being difficult, but will comply anyway.

Comment: "I hated it." (When the plate is empty.)
Snappy answer: "Har har har!"

Truth: We've heard that one a million times, sorry.

INDEXES
By Restaurant and Town

ABOUT THE AUTHORS

Matthew DeLaMater is an editor, publisher, ghost writer, and author with a deep attachment to the Adirondack region that formed in the summers of his youth. A sometime resident of Long Lake, he has managed to survive a few winters there. DeLaMater is the lead author of the featured reviews found in this book, though hardly the sole contributor.

Molly Irvine lives in the Saratoga region where she teaches full-time. Her family, a noted collection of eccentrics, has been spending summers here in Long Lake since the turn of the century. Having worked extensively in local restaurants and bars, Molly has a sympathetic insider's take to evaluating the local cuisine. Molly's gregarious nature and insights into the region were vital in preparing the local surveys.

Food Snob for astute reasons, has chosen to remain anonymous. His extensive dining experiences both locally and abroad provide some broader contextualization for evaluating the Adirondack dining experience. A consultant to many chefs, Food Snob is an innovative cook in his own right, and has a secret fantasy to run his own place (as long as it isn't terribly hard work). The majority of Food Snob's snotty remarks were stricken from this book in order to protect him, but a few made it to press in order to placate him.